TEE BALL TO-A-TEE ™

TEE BALL Coaching Handbook

A Comprehensive guide to coaching tee ball teams whether you're a first-time coach or a seasoned pro.

FOREWORD

COACHING PHILOSOPHY

Successful coaches teach players how to play the game properly. They develop players' self-

esteem and confidence by helping them succeed at the sport. Whether you are a parent, a first-year coach or a veteran coach, learning how to apply your knowledge will enhance your abilities to teach. Everyone's level of baseball knowledge is different. Our common goal as coaches is our desire to help our kids or players on the team we coach become better players.

The better a coach or parent understands the fundamentals, the better these skills can be taught to the young player. Understanding the fundamentals is an important ingredient of being a coach, but only one ingredient.

If you are unable to communicate knowledge to your players, that knowledge is wasted. How knowledge is communicated to the player is an important factor in becoming a successful coach. Two things always take place when coaching is effective. First, the players fully understand what the coach is saying. Second, the players are able to apply their new knowledge. Getting players to understand the point you are attempting to make is the easier of the two, but still should not be taken for granted. Helping the players apply their new knowledge can be a challenge, and this ultimately is the deciding factor of whether the coach is successful and the players have learned.

If a coach tells a player he is doing a particular skill incorrectly, and the player continues to do it incorrectly, the coach is not communicating effectively. Breaking the information down into small "bites" combined with correct demonstration of the skill is the most effective way for a young player to learn. Players who are taught the correct fundamental skills and develop a positive attitude have the best chance for success. Repetition and a player's aptitude and desire to learn will ultimately determine success.

When coaching players who are still developing mentally and physically, focus on teaching them the fundamentally correct way to perform each skill. If coaches can encourage players to repeat these fundamentals correctly, give the players positive reinforcement, then allow the player the freedom to perform, players will have more success at the skill they are trying to develop, and will have FUN in the process.

TABLE OF CONTENTS

TEE BALL TO-A-TEE

Tips For TeeBall Parents

General Tips For parents to help them determine if their child is ready to play tee ball and help both parent and child to enjoy the experience.

If you are a coach, you should share these ideas with the parents on your team. You may copy and distribute these pages freely with your team information.

A. Make sure your child is ready for Tee Ball.

Obviously, this is the most fundamental element of whether you and your child enjoy the tee ball experience. Many children play tee ball (as well as many other sports) simply because their parents want them to play. Children **WANT** to please their parents, so naturally they will usually do what their parents wish whether they want to or not.

> 1.   Ask yourself: Does my child even WANT to play tee ball?
> 2.   Is he/she physically/mentally ready for an organized sport?

If the answer to either of these questions is no, it is better to wait until next year, simply because of the level of interest and safety concerns.

B. Assuming your child is ready and wants to play, what must you, as a parent do to help get them ready to play?

Long before the first practice, spend some time in preparation. Begin by making the experience a fun and learning one. The best way is to begin teaching without the child even realizing that he or she is being taught - so it doesn't become "work." Indulge in the pure enjoyment of "having a catch" with your child. This is great fun for you and your child, and will lay the foundation for many enjoyable hours later on. In "having a catch," you are teaching the proper way to catch and throw the ball. As your child's skill level improves, you (and they) will begin making more difficult throws and catches.

In addition to "having a catch," playing "wiffle ball" is a great (and inexpensive) way to begin developing batting skills. Developing the hand/eye skills necessary for batting is vital to success and satisfaction. Take a moment at the outset to demonstrate the proper grip, batting stance and swing. Don't allow yourself to become frustrated if it takes awhile for your child to grasp the concepts you present. That is the surest way to kill the desire to learn.

Whatever you do, give lots of praise and encouragement when warranted. The surest way to speed up the learning process is to praise when your young player gives solid effort and executes a procedure well. They will work extra hard to earn more praise. If they struggle, take a break, get a treat, have a little conversation, and come back later. Sometimes a little time off does wonders.

C. Get the right kind of equipment for your young player.

1. GLOVE.

Pick a glove that is the right size for your child's hand. Don't get one that is too small, and don't get one that is too big, thinking "(s)he'll grow into it." It is more likely the glove will be too much for him/her to handle now, while (s)he's learning.

Do NOT get a cheap plastic or vinyl glove. Invest a little more and get a glove made of real leather. It will be better in the long run. If you get the right size, he/she will be able to use the glove for several years. You can get a satisfactory glove for $25 or $30.

2. BAT.

Again, pick the right size and weight. If the bat is too heavy, your young player just won't be able to manage it. If it is too long, ditto. An aluminum bat that is 15-16 ounces is the best weight, and around 25- 26 inches in length. You should be able to get a good bat for around $25 or $30.

3. SHOES WITH CLEATS.

It's a good idea to get cleats from the beginning.

It's good practice for them to learn running in them. Cleats also provide better traction to prevent slipping, unlike slick-bottomed tennis shoes.

D.   Set realistic goals and expectations.

Consider for a moment that your child may not be the best player on the team. Consider that he/she may not be the least skilled player on the team either.

Regardless of where your child falls in the spectrum of talent, your expectations must be consistent with his/her abilities. While some children will perform beyond their parents' wildest expectations, some will fall short of what their parents expect. Whatever the case, make sure that your expectations fall within the realm of what your child can accomplish. Often a child that struggles early on, but if given the proper training and encouragement, will shine in subsequent years. If the game remains fun, the chances for success and enjoyment increase. If it becomes a chore or an embarrassment, the chances are, that the child will regress or quit entirely.

E.   Expect and maintain an open dialogue with your child's coach(es).

Ask questions. Have certain expectations of your coaches. What does your coach expect of the team and its players during the season? What goals does the coach have for your child? If your coach does something you don't like - express it to him or her in a calm, reasonable manner. (Most) Coaches expect questions and truly appreciate valid feedback from parents. However, no one appreciates an antagonistic approach at the outset; so find common ground with your coach and meet him there.

F.   Have fun! It's a great game - enjoy it!

Cheer, laugh, and whoop it up! These are great years, and you can create some truly wonderful memories for a lifetime.

TEE BALL TO-A-TEE

The First Five Minutes

(of Practice Are The Most Important)

Learn how the first five minutes of teeball practice can set the tone for success... and FUN!

The First Five Minutes (of practice are the most important)

The first five minutes of your TeeBall practice may be the most important five minutes of your team's time together. The first five minutes set the tone for what can be a fantastic, fun-filled practice or a confusing, boring exercise in futility.

Much of what follows those introductory five minutes, will be determined by how well you assess your team's mood, and how much you do as coach to directly influence it in a positive way.

HERE ARE FIVE WAYS TO MAKE THE FIRST FIVE MINUTES OF PRACTICE COUNT:

MINUTE 1. Take a minute to address each of them by name.

It is a great thrill for your players to know that you know them by name. Likewise, they realize how unimportant they are if you refer to them as "Hey, kid!" It may take a practice or two before you recognize them and can identify them easily, but it is well worth the effort.

The First Five Minutes (of practice are the most important)

MINUTE 2. Have a Plan.
Explain your Plan.

Give them something to look forward to. Take a minute to explain what your team will be doing today. Do a good sales job here and they will jump through hoops for you. "Guys, today we're going to learn how to run the bases the right way, and we're going to learn how to field a baseball using a "Gator." This always raises the level of curiosity, as everybody wants to know, "A REAL Alligator, Coach?" "We're also going to learn how to get runners out at first and second base, we're going to learn how to catch a pop fly, and we're going to see who can 'Catch the Coach.' Are you ready to have some fun and play ball?"

MINUTE 3. Got a kind word to say?
Say it!

Who knows what little Johnny went through at school today? Maybe he had a fight with his sister - and she won. Maybe he's in a little trouble with Mom or Dad. Maybe the kind words you say will be the only ones he hears all week. Take a minute to find something positive to say.

The First Five Minutes (of practice are the most important)

 MINUTE 4. Look pleasant.

The kids could care less how motivated you are to win the Tee Ball Championship this year. They, on the other hand, are incredibly motivated by the snacks that will be handed out at the end of practice. If they sense too much frustration on the part of their coach or parents, they will sometimes "shut down" or "check out." Expect them to have difficulty grasping some concepts - **they're 4, 5 and 6 years old!** A pleasant disposition is crucial. It will help YOU when they are struggling to master something, and it will help **THEM** if they sense that "Coach thinks I can do this." If your players sense that you would rather be pulling your own teeth than coaching them, it won't be long before you'll wish you were. Take a minute to let your face say you're glad to be there.

The First Five Minutes (of practice are the most important)

MINUTE 5. Engage them in a fun drill or activity right away.

Find a drill or game that they seem to enjoy, and let them do it first thing out of the gate. It should be something that loosens them up and gets them into the right frame of mind in a fun way. This will get them into your corner quickly and get them ready for more focused activity later. It is also a good idea to do another fun drill about halfway through the practice as a reward for good effort. Take a minute to make it fun for them (and YOU!).

We sometimes forget that our little players come to us fresh from a day of school or other activities, fueled with lots of energy (fueled by sugar), excited to see their buddies, and ready for fun! Sometimes, however, they are ready for anything **BUT** TeeBall. They see something special in every plane passing overhead, every crawling bug, even in a pile of dirt and rocks.

As coaches, it is our task to draw them into the game, find joy in playing as a team, and instill in them an excitement for playing and enjoying the great sport of baseball.

TEE BALL TO-A-TEE

12 Things You REALLY Need To Know About Coaching Tee Ball!

Here's a dozen REALLY helpful hints to help in coaching your child's tee ball team!

12 Things You REALLY Need To Know About Coaching Tee Ball

1

Organize. Plan. Execute.

You wouldn't take off on a cross-country trip without a road map would you? Well, neither should you embark on a TeeBall season without a plan. Take some time before the season starts to decide **WHAT** you want to accomplish, **HOW** you want to do it, and **WHY** you want to do it. Make sure you're in this coaching tee ball thing for the "right reasons." What are the "right reasons?" Write down five reasons you want to coach a tee ball team and read it to your child. You'll know.

(HINT: "To Have Fun" MUST be in the top five.)

HAVE A PLAN!

2

Teeballers (ages 4-6) Typically Have Shorter Attention Spans.

With organization comes many benefits. Organized practices allow you to make the most out of any practice times that you have together. Plan your practice times so that you minimize any standing around. If they are active and having fun they are more apt to be focused during practice. **KEEP THEM BUSY!**

12 Things You REALLY Need To Know About Coaching Tee Ball

3

Make Tee Ball A Fun Experience.

This should be true for you and the kids. You'll be surprised how focused they will be for a one hour practice if games are used to teach skills or if they know something special is coming at the end of practice. Ice cream treats are a great way to reward good effort by youngsters. They get a real feeling of accomplishment knowing they have pleased the coach, and done a good job. Sometimes it's beneficial to do something special even after a frustrating practice.
BE CREATIVE!

4

Keep Expectations Realistic.

You're probably going to have between 12-14 kids on your team. The best you can hope for is that half of them will understand the game fairly well by the end of the season, and if that's the case, thank your lucky stars. Don't expect to take your team and "whip them into a finely-tuned offensive and defensive machine." Anticipate teaching key skills, developing players and keeping them from getting hurt.
SEE IT FOR WHAT IT IS!

5

Keep Your Practices Short And Skill-Focused.

Don't try to cram too much information into a short practice. Remember the ancient Chinese proverb about how to eat an elephant - "one bite at a time." Smaller bits of information are easier for these young minds to process and retain. **SIMPLIFY!**

6

Don't Assume They Know What You Mean.

Not all children know where the bases are or where right field is. Most likely, they probably won't remember from practice to practice, so be prepared to show them again and again. **ASSUME NOTHING.**

7

Young Children Are Very Literal.

If you are about to execute a baserunning drill from home to second base, make sure they understand what you expect. If you tell them to run from home base to second, don't be surprised if they take off across the pitcher's mound in a straight line towards second base. **DEMONSTRATE!**

12 Things You REALLY Need To Know About Coaching Tee Ball

8

Express Your Goals To The Parents.

The single most important thing that you can do is clearly communicate your goals and expectations to the parents. Most will be concerned only if they perceive your coaching style as "the-win-at-all-costs-type." If they know you will help their child get somewhat better, that you will treat him/her fairly, and that you will provide a positive influence, they will be absolutely thrilled. **COMMUNICATE!**

9

Get Help.

No, we're not saying as in "professional help". Involve your parents. Get as many parents as you possibly can involved in the practice and game process. When a person accepts a position of Team Helper or Assistant Coach, two things happen:

1.)   You'll have more help.

       (Trust us, you'll need it!)

2.)   They are less likely to be critical.

PROMOTE PARTICIPATION.

10

Laugh A Lot.

Laugh with them, not <u>at</u> them. If the kids see you enjoying yourself, chances are pretty good, they will too. An uptight, screaming coach does little to foster a positive attitude. It does nothing to improve their skills and develop them as a player. What it does do is give you, and those around you a headache.

ENJOY THE OPPORTUNITY YOU ARE GIVEN!

11

Promote Good Sportsmanship.

Do not permit temper tantrums on your part, on the kids' part, on your assistant coaches' part, or on your parents' part.

TEACH BY EXAMPLE.

12

Be The Person They Remember (Positively) Twenty Years From Now.

Chances are, each of us remembers a coach or teacher from our past, that we recall fondly. It is also highly likely that we can recall at least one individual that causes us to inwardly cringe when we remember our experience with them. Strive to be a pleasant memory, and a positive influence.

BUILD MEMORIES!

TEE BALL TO-A-TEE ™

Coaching Tee Ball: General Practice Guidelines

Here's a position-by-position breakdown of the skills you'll need to develop in your players as a successful Tee Ball coach.

Most new coaches are understandably nervous about the prospect of taking on a group of hyperactive, energetic 4-6 year olds and molding them into something that resembles a team. While realistic expectations are essential, it is also good to establish goals that will allow them to develop their abilities, have fun and put in place a foundation that will allow them to improve and develop a genuine love for the game.

The following guidelines are suggested as a review for new coaches. It is equally valid as a reference for experienced coaches.

REMEMBER: Break learning experiences into small "bites" of information and instruction so that even the youngest player can understand and retain.

First Base

Demonstrate where 1st baseman is to stand (typically about 3-4 feet off first base and either in front of or behind the runner).
Actually practice fielding plays; have ball thrown to first base by various infielders to initiate the "play."

Second Base

Position player in place, anticipating action. Practice fielding plays; such as tagging a runner out.

Shortstop

Show position between 2B and 3B.
Practice action; such as fielding balls and throwing to first base or 2B for an out.

Third Base

Show position, anticipating action. Practice action - such as player moving in front of the ball.

Pitcher

(Stands in pitcher's area but acts as an infielder.) Practice action - such as fielding ball and throwing to first base.

Catcher

Stands behind and away from home plate until ball is hit.

Demonstrate: after ball is hit, adult removes tee and bat; catcher moves up to cover plate.

Practice: catcher tagging baserunner out, catcher throwing to first base.

General infield activity

In "Ready Position" anticipating the ball to be hit to them.

Catching short fly balls.

Field balls and throwing to a base or to home plate.

Tagging runners on the basepath.

Relaying a ball from an outfielder to a base; to the catcher at home plate.

Outfielders

Generally there are five or more outfielders in TeeBall

Position players where you wish them to stand.

Practice catching fly balls in a crowd. Call out, "I've got it!"

Practice catching ground balls and throwing to infield.

Have one outfielder receive relay from another and throw to an infielder.

Batter

Give basic hitting instructions. Show basic stance and grip - don't get fancy here - remember you need to keep it simple. Encourage a strong swing.

Practice hitting the ball, dropping the bat properly, then running to first.

Base Runners

Instruct actions at first base.   (Coach at first base signals to run past base or to turn and go on to 2B.)

Instruct that forced runner on base must advance.

Non-forced runner can hold position on base.

Player on base must watch what next batter does; where the ball goes.

Bench

Team sits in batting order. (Ask the dugout parent to put tape with the player's name in a position on the bench and instruct them that they are to be sitting in that spot. The team should be encouraging the batter when they are not on deck or batting).

NO BATS IN DUGOUT! EVER!

When the coach talks - listen for instructions.

Coach (post-game):

Summarize team's activity. Offer specifics, not generalities - accentuate the positive. Recognize progress. Note any humorous or exciting thing that happened. Stress playing fair by the rules and having fun.

If one-on-one comments are necessary (instruction, discipline, etc.), take player aside.

Other comments, as appropriate.

HITTING

Batting — Demonstrate stance, swing and follow-through.
Proper technique is important!
Adjust the tee with ball set even to the hitter's waist.
*(Some leagues have the coach pitch three pitches befoer setting up the tee
- if you can teach a player to hit the pitch - Excellent!)*
Face tee with feet spread shoulder-width apart.

> Bend knees, body in slight crouch.
> Weight on balls of feet.
> Grip bat; hands together above knob.
> Bring bat up and away from the body.
> Keep shoulders level; bat and head steady.
> Eyes on the ball.
> Short step towards pitcher with the front foot at start of swing.
> Swing level and bring the bat through the center of the ball.
> Watch bat hit ball; keep head down.
> Weight shifts to front foot; back foot stays on the ground.
> Extend arms and follow through; swing around.
> Drop the bat; do not throw it.

KEY POINTS:
eyes on the ball
no cross-handed grip
position of feet
stride [weight shift]
rotation
the swing

Don't complicate - SIMPLIFY!

FIELDING

Instruct players to keep eyes on the ball.

Watch the ball go into the glove.

Cover the ball with the other hand.

GROUND BALL

Stand legs apart, shoulder-width or wider.

Bend knees. Get low. Lean forward.

Run to the ball.

Keep body in front of ball.

Glove low to the ground.

Scoop or catch the ball and cover it with the other hand.

FLY BALL

Run to where the ball is going.

Call for the ball: "I've got it." - **LOUD!**

Stop and wait for the ball.

Hands together, fingers up, shoulder high or over the head -
    not blocking view of ball.

Watch ball into the glove and cover with the other hand.

CATCHING THE THROWN BALL

Bend knees slightly watch the ball into glove.

On a ball thrown to player above the waist:

Hands together facing out; thumbs up.

Catch and cover.

On a ball thrown below the waist:

Hands together facing down; little fingers touching.

Catch and cover.

THROWING

Demonstrate grip and motion.

Thumb under the ball.

Two or three fingers on top.

Don't worry about the seams.

Eyes on the target.

Legs apart; foot on throwing arm side behind the body.

Arm back and up, front shoulder turned toward target.

Step toward target with the foot opposite the throwing arm
(Right-hander lead with left foot; left-hander lead with right foot).

Push off on back foot as throw begins; end with weight on forward foot.

Release the ball in front of body and follow through.

RUNNING

BASE RUNNING

Run on the balls of the feet. Pump arms back and forth.

After the ball is hit:

Do not run into the tee.

Look at first base, not where the ball has gone.

Run outside the foul line.

Run straight through first base; peel to right unless instructed otherwise; do not slow down.

Watch and listen to coach for instructions.

When on base:

Keep one foot touching the base until the next batter hits the ball.

Lean forward; when ball is hit, push off base.

Know where the ball is.

When passing a base, try to touch it on the corner without stopping.

SLIDING

(Not recommended for the youngest players)

It is recommended that this skill be attempted only with players of the appropriate skill level. As such, many tee ball leagues even discourage sliding.

If it is allowed in your park's system, here's a few "sliding pointers"

Start about four to five feet from the base.

Arms up, fingers bent, chin down.

Bend one leg under the other.

Lower leg hits the ground, then the butt and back.

Top leg (the extended one) touches the base - on the corner.

No head-first sliding.

No pop-up slides.

TEE BALL TO-A-TEE ™

A Great Beginning TeeBall Practice Routine

Want to organize the first practice for your TeeBall team?
Here it is –
a plan for starting your season out right!

1

Warm up.

Have everyone run twice around the bases. Show them how to touch the inside corner of the base.

2

Stretch.

As they stretch, have them count out loud to "TEN!" as loudly as they can. They really have fun with that - especially trying to out-yell each other.

3

Go over the positions...

… so they learn the name of each one. Run from position to position as a group, "Who knows what position this is?" "Who plays this position for our team?" You will be surprised how quickly they learn this when they do it as a group - plus, they get a real kick out of it.

4

Split into 2 groups.

Divide them into groups A & B - you can't effectively teach skills to 13 kids at a time.

5

Take group A and practice:
Drills are done one at a time.

a.   Hit the ball, DROP THE BAT, and run to first.

Do this twice with each player. It gives you a chance to personally assess their swing. Do this for a few practices until they get it down.

A Great Beginning Tee Ball Practice Routine

b.   Throwing - set up targets.

Use soft plastic office trash cans. You can stack up two or three and use this as their "throwing target". This will most likely be their favorite drill. Use this time to work on the correct mechanics of throwing.

c.   Use bucket drills for catching, fielding technique, and more throwing practice.

You (or one of your assistants) take a big bucket - two players take two smaller buckets. Each player should be rolled grounders or thrown to until all the balls in the big bucket are uased. After players catch the ball, they put the balls into a smaller bucket. The other players awaiting turns retrieve any missed balls and put them into the smaller buckets. When your bucket is empty you refill from the already collected balls in the smaller buckets and go to two different players. This drill allows more repetitions to improve each player's skill. You can instruct and correct them in between each one. Start with tennis balls for catching until you are sure they won't hold their gloves palm up at head level causing the ball to bounce out of their glove and into their face. You need another adult "helper" to keep the kids in some semblence of order during this drill.

A Great Beginning Tee Ball Practice Routine

d.   Infield practice - the basics of infield.

Start out by just making the play at first. Don't worry about the other bases until they get that down.

6

Group B does hitting and skills
Drills are done one at a time.

a.   Set up 3 tees and hit wiffle balls into a fence or net.

You need 2-3 parents to run the tees. If parents are reticent to help here, bring some pamphlets on basic batting stance, etc. or have a quick "this is the basics of what the kids should be doing at the tee" clinic for the parents who may be interested.

b.   Remaining Group B kids go to skill station

Here players practice basic throwing, catching, maybe pop flies, or make up a few fun games. It helps tremendously if you get volunteer parents to assist at the skill station.

c.   Kids rotate through 2 stations.

7

Switch Groups A & B after 20 minutes or so.

(Assuming a one hour practice)

8 **Leave the last 15 minutes of practice for a one-inning scrimmage.**

Group A vs B to practice the skills they've just learned.

9 **You will find your players' skills increasing after several practices.**

Focus on basic throwing and fielding grounders the first few practices.

10 **Explain your practice format to the parents at the beginning of the first practice or team meeting.**

Tell them you will need "___" number of parents to make this format work so the kids will have fun and not wind up standing around getting bored.

11 **Be patient.**

You may have to repeat something to these young players 10 times before they hear you. Have fun and NO YELLING!!

12 **Hope for helpful parents.**

Your job will be much easier and it will increase the parents' and children's enjoyment immensely!

TEE BALL TO-A-TEE

TEEBALL COACHING TIPS TO THE RESCUE!

How can you survive the season coaching a TeeBall team? Here's a simple step-by-step plan to not only survive, but make it a great experience for you AND your team!

COACHING TIPS TO THE RESCUE

1. Get organized, develop a plan, and prepare to work hard.
Learn as much about TeeBall and baseball as you can. Prepare to learn enough about baseball to be able to present the material in "kid terms."

2. Kids don't know a lot of terms you take for granted.
They don't know what it means to "step in the bucket" or "take an extra base" or "turn two" until you teach them and show them. Successful coaches know their audience and use analogies and common visual imagery to establish a connection with their players. For TeeBall players, these images are best when they are a bit dramatic: "point the belly button toward the part of the field where you want to hit the ball (get your hips rotated), make your arm like an elephant's trunk when throwing (don't launch the ball like a catapult, THROW it), and point the button on your cap in the direction the ball came from when fielding a ground ball (keep your head down)", for instance.

3. Whether your league keeps score or not, or whether you have a team that can win games or not, don't ever fail to take your responsibilities as a coach seriously.
Being a serious coach means that you'll try to teach them something about baseball, basic skills, and sportsmanship. It means that you're attentive to player safety. It also means that while you're asking your players to put their best foot forward, so are you.

4. Having been a good player is no assurance that you will be a good coach any more than being a good student necessarily means you will be a good teacher.
A coach must possess certain qualities – many coaches are satisfied with merely having characteristics. A coach has to be a good teacher, he has to be patient, he has to be confident and decisive, he has to be nurturing when his players get hurt or make mistakes, and he has to be able to get as much as he can out of his players without going too far.

5. Tell players' parents that TeeBall is NOT just like the game of baseball.

It's just different and they need to know the difference so that their expectations will be realistic and consistent with skill level. For example, there is no leading off, no stealing, etc.

6. Try not to be partial to your own child.

If you can do it, try to be a coach on the field and a parent off the field, and get your fellow coaches to do the same. Impartiality (and avoiding excessive impartiality) is essential to success.

7. Coaches need the assistance of their players' parents.

Parents are normally willing to help out if they aren't too busy. They tend to learn that the more they participate in the operation of the team, the more they also stay in touch with the challenges coaches encounter as they try to build the team. Getting parents' assistance does not mean losing control of the team to them.

8. There can be three hundred people in the stands and three coaches shouting during a game, but the one voice a player hears is his own parents'.

This isn't a problem until the coach tells the player to stop and the parent yells for him to go. The only thing a coach can do about this is tell the parents how tough it is to communicate with the players when there are conflicting instructions on the field. At times, it can be a safety issue.

9. Parents bring their own expectations into the season and it's safe to assume that coaches and managers do the same.

The best way to ensure there are no surprises as the season develops is for the manager to hold a meeting and set the tone early. He should let the parents know that he knows what he is doing and what he is going to do. This helps them develop confidence in him during this first team meeting.

10. The only way to build a good team out of a group of individuals is through effective practice.

On the field, you have to be a teacher as well as a coach. Teach them what they need to know, show them what you taught them, practice the things you taught them over and over, then be prepared to do it all over again.

11. Practice, by definition, presumes repetition.

Repetition is the keystone of successful game preparation. However, repetition soon turns into monotony with players, particularly TeeBall players, unless you: (1) PLAN every aspect of every practice right down to the minute, (2) Keep your practices ORGANIZED and MOVING, and (3) Make a GAME out of as many things as you can.

12. Remember that players will not perform effectively in games unless they have practiced that way.

If you don't practice base running, you will get base running outs in games. If you don't drill the players on catching the ball and making a good, smart throw, they won't do it in the game. Attention to the basics is essential. Conversely, your expectations must be realistically consistent with the skill level of the player.

13. To make the most of your practice time, break the team up into two or three groups, depending on the number of coaches, space, and equipment you have available for the workout.

This will enable you to accomplish two or three times as much work without making players stand around with nothing to do.

14. Proper dugout behavior is essential to good order on the ball-field during the game.

As with all other elements of the practice, if you don't achieve it in practice, you won't achieve it in the game. A dugout full of hyenas is very distracting to the team and the coaches. It also sets the tone for what will happen between the baselines.

15. As you're working with your TeeBall players, try to avoid letting hitters stand nearly motionless in one position in the batter's box too long.

When a hitter stands in one place too long, he tends to settle vertically in his stance while he's waiting to swing. This makes it difficult for him to transfer this momentum horizontally into his hitting motion.

16. Whatever the coach does with foot positioning during the hitting sequence, he must ensure the hitter maintains control over his power and balance and can reach the ball with the "sweet" part of the bat.

As the stride is begun with the batter's weight and head back over the back foot and weight on the balls of the feet, the hitter transfers his weight in the swing with the head kept back behind the point of contact with the ball. Pay close attention to where and how your hitter stands in the batter's box. Many coaches simply let their hitters approach the tee and start flailing away at the ball.

17. If you've spent any time around TeeBall at all, you've seen coaches who framed their entire offensive strategy around a scheme to have hitters challenge the outfield's ability to catch the ball by hitting pop flies.

However, when the level of competition elevates or when players get older, those deep fly balls turn into disappointing outs. Teams score a lot of runs just by hitting hard grounders and crisp line drives through holes in the defense. TeeBall players can place-hit, if shown how.

18. Teach your players to slide (safely).

It makes the game safer, it can help them avoid a high tag, and it keeps them on the base when you don't want them to wander off of it.ONLY do this in games if they master this skill in practice.

19. One of the most common, yet subtle hazards to players involves the handling of bats by players waiting to bat.

Let it be your team policy that a player doesn't handle a bat unless a coach hands it to him. Once a coach hands a player a bat, let him maintain the player in his supervision.

20. The most common mistake parents make when they're teaching their kids to catch pop flies is that they don't make sure they get to the ball before they try to catch it.
Teach kids to catch pop flies in two steps: run and center up under the ball, then put your glove up and catch the ball. Of course, there are times when the player can't center up, but you need to start with teaching to catch the easy fly ball first.

REALLY BAD, NOT FUN, AWFUL SCENARIOS
Survival Guide For Tee Ball Coaches

HOW TO:

- ☞ Deal With Parents
- ☞ Handle Unresponsive/Unruly/ Tempermental/Disruptive/Shy, etc., etc. Players
- ☞ Assist Very Low-Skilled Players
- ☞ Much More!

Really Bad, Awful, Not Fun Scenarios - Survival For Tee Ball Coaches

Your absolute worst coaching nightmare has been realized.

You've just returned from your first TeeBall team practice.

Not one of the kids on your team has even the slightest clue as to what the game is about. Okay - (deep breath) you can deal with that. That's why you signed up to coach, right? To teach kids to play baseball. It'll be fun. Really, you can do this.

But that dad that screamed at his son the whole time - whoa!

And the mom who threatened legal action if her daughter didn't get to play pitcher "because it was important for her self-esteem". (By the way, the little girl did NOT want to play pitcher.)

And the guy who said he didn't mind where you played his son as long as it was pitcher, short, second or first, and he batted first every game and he said he was just kidding … hehehehehehe…
(He wasn't kidding).

Don't laugh. While you may not have it THAT bad, chances are, during the season, you may encounter some problem that may really throw you for a loop. And when you do encounter that unexpected dilemma or problem, you should deal with it quickly and effectively to limit its potential negative impact on your team and the positive experience you want to establish.

Please note that while these examples may prove to be extreme, they are representative of the KINDS of problems you may encounter. It is not possible to discuss all "worst case sceanrios" in this handbook (you'd never take the time to read it if it did!). What we've tried to present are possible situations that may arise, and how they can be dealt with.

* SPECIAL NOTE: If you have a "Really Bad, Awful, Not Fun Scenario" that you'd like to share, please e-mail the situation and (if you had one) the solution you utilized to us at *headcoach@teeball-to-a-tee.com.* We'd love to share the input in future updates of our "Coaching Handbook."

Really Bad, Awful, Not Fun Scenarios - Survival For Tee Ball Coaches

1. Your First Practice Was A Disaster. Everything was so unorganized.
   You know, Rome wasn't built in a day and neither are good TeeBall teams. Most TeeBall teams will typically consist of 12 - 14 kids, all with a million questions and all charged with limitless energy. If your first practice was a "disaster", chances were, the organization of the practice left something to be desired.
   Quickest Solution? Next practice, take a written practice schedule with drills broken down into timed segments with definite parameters. Be prepared to have fun, but be firm enough to expect respect and effort.
   TeeBall-To-A-Tee offers our Practice In A Pocket System© (P.I.P.S.) to help you organize and plan a great practice. You can order it at www.teeball-to-a-tee.com.

2. You Couldn't Get the Kids' Attention.
   This will get better as they get further along in the season and they come to understand the expectations that you, the other coaches, the parents, and their teammates have for them. It is very important however, that you get and hold their attention quickly so you don't waste valuable practice time.
   Quickest Solution? Line everybody up and do a couple minutes minutes of warm-up exercises. You might even take a lap around the field with your players trailing along behind you screaming out some team chant that you've made up (use your imagination, here). Be funny and fun for a few minutes, and then ask, "All right everybody ready to learn how to be better baseball players?" By this time, you should get exuberant shouts of "Ready, Coach!"

3. One Kid (or more) Is Being Disruptive Enough For The Whole Team.
   You can't seem to get them to behave and stop interfering with the other kids.
   This can get out of hand in a hurry, and if you don't deal with it properly, it can pose a problem for you and your team during your entire season. Make a quick analysis of the situation, and mentally isolate the cause(s) of the problem.
   Quickest Solution? If it is between a couple of players, discreetly isolate them from one another. (You might simply separate them by placing them in separate stations). If the problem persists, you might have the trouble maker(s) sit on the bench for five minutes. Typically, this will solve the problem as they will see their buddies running around and having fun and will want to be part of the action. At this point, you should tell them that if they continue to misbehave, they won't be able to do some of the fun things the rest of the team is doing. If it continues to persist after that, you might address the issue with the parents in a non-confrontational one- on-one discussion. Explain your actions, and what you are trying to do for the benefit of the entire team and enlist their assistance in dealing with the problem. Usually this nips most behavioral problems in the bud.

Really Bad, Awful, Not Fun Scenarios - Survival For Tee Ball Coaches

4. Then you may say, "I did what you said in #3, and the dad said he was going to kick my butt if I did it again."

You laugh, but this could happen.

Quickest Solution? If this does happen, try to explain to the dad (again) what you are trying to accomplish for the good of the entire team. If his eyes glaze over and he still makes threatening comments about inflicting physical punishment, then simply ask if he will help you coach drills with his son. If he balks at this, then explain that you want to help his son get better, but that you need his help to help him realize his full potential.

If he's still antagonistic - you'll just have to plan a way to include his son in the drills and instruction process while keeping him from interrupting the flow of your practice. This is usually a good time to break them into even smaller groups and have the troublemaker(s) virtually one-on-one with a parent helper (or you if necessary).

A NOTE ASIDE:

While in many ways the scenario described above may seem almost humorous, be assured that you should never take threats from any parent, guardian, spectator or fellow coach lightly. We are all too familiar with incidents of violence in youth sports which seem to dominate the news today. If a situation arises, immediately do all you can to resolve the issue quietly, and peacefully, and report the transgressor to your league officials, the umpire (if during a game) or even the local authorities if necessary.

5. A parent (not a parent helper and not a coach) berates his child the majority of the time during practice and games. The poor kid is confused, frustrated and so afraid he/she doesn't know what to do.

And the sad thing is, the parent obviously thinks this helps their child perform better.

Quickest Solution? When this happens, it is a good plan to discreetly position the child as far away from the parent during a practice or game. Failing that, quietly ask the parent one-on-one if they would relax a little bit and cut their own child some slack (My words here, use your discretion and good judgement). Explain that you know that little Johnny needs some work in some areas, but that he really is doing pretty well considering he's only five. Add that you and the other coaches will continue to try and help him improve, but that if he could do you a personal favor, and only be positive in his comments. **Be tactful & diplomatic!**

6. **You've got 4-5 players (out of 13) who are pretty good. The others are basically clueless. The parents of the better kids are pressuring you to let the better kids play in the infield the whole time so you can "win" (The scoreboard is never turned on). You've been trying to move the kids around, and teach them to play different positions. What do you do?**
You have to wonder how the parents of the "better" kids would view this if their kid were the less skilled one.
Quickest Solution? Keep doing what you're doing, but explain to the parents that what you are trying to do is teach the kids to play different positions so that:
A.) They will know what positions they LIKE to play.
B.) They can learn different skills
C.) They will learn to appreciate the game
D.) It's TeeBall, for Pete's sake, let 'em have fun - it gets serious enough later on.
BUT, DO THIS. Make sure that through your ongoing evaluation process of the players you determine which infield positions they are most capable of playing.
In other words, you as a coach should **MAXIMIZE** their chances for success and **MINIMIZE** their chances for failure.

7. **One of your coaches, parents, parent helpers (whatever) is going around behind your back bad-mouthing you to the other parents, criticizing my coaching style and generally being unsupportive. What should you do?**
What would be so hard about this person coming to you directly and working through this together in a mature way? Now YOU have to do the hard part.
Quickest Solution? Approach the person in a non-threatening environment (as in not in front of the whole team and parents - perhaps meet him/her for lunch), and ask if there is some way the two of you could work better together. Explain that you want to do the best job you can as a coach and that you would appreciate some constructive input. People appreciate positive handling of any situation (even if they've initiated it). In this way, it may be possible for the two of you to arrive at some things that you can do to mutually benefit the team and each other.

8. **One (or more) of the kids on your team is extremely uncoordinated and clumsy. They don't seem to be "getting it." You can't seem to get them to complete and master the drills and skill-building exercises at the same rate as the others. It's making it difficult for you to teach them the proper skills and coach effectively.**
Kids simply mature and develop at different rates. Today's clumsy, uncoordinated TeeBall player may be tomorrow's superstar (and vice versa). If you had a team full of superstars - where's the challenge (and fun) in that?

Really Bad, Awful, Not Fun Scenarios - Survival For Tee Ball Coaches

Quickest Solution? Be P-A-T-I-E-N-T and work with all kids on your team at a level commiserate with their ability. You may be on the path to developing a youngster who will become a great player, a good player, or simply a kid who will love the game of baseball. Obviously, you will have to work harder with the less-skilled players, but the end result will be worth it, when they come up and thank you ten years from now and proudly and affectionately call you "Coach."

9. **HELP! I've gotten in over my head and you have no idea how to handle all these kids, parents, granparents, and deal with their expectations. I don't have any assistant coaches at this point, and no one's stepped forward to help.**
   The biggest fear most TeeBall coaches have is just that - they will not be up to the task and they won't have the help they need. This is NOT the major leagues here, and MOST people are willing to help if given the right role to fill.
   Quickest Solution? Ask for help from your group of parents (not in front of the kids). Explain that you are a little overwhelmed and while you have a plan for the season (review the other sections of this handbook), you need a little help in certain areas to make the season a successful and fun one. In order to do this how ever, you will need an outline that you can share with them. Take a few minutes before your meeting and outline your five (or whatever the number is - keep it manageable - you don't want to scare them off!) greatest needs. Ask for a volunteer(s) to handle a particular area and assign responsibilities. You will be surprised at how much help you can get if you ask for it.

10. **I've got a parent that insists that it would be better if I assigned each player a position and let them play that position all year. He feels that this is the only way they will learn and get better.**
    Oddly enough, (wink, wink) this comment probably comes from a parent who considers his kid as one of the "better" players and assumes he/she will be featured in one of the "prime" positions.
    Quickest Solution? Indicate that you think that's a great idea! Ask if they are prepared to have their child play outfield the whole season if that's what you decide to do, and you determine that is the player's best position and chance for success. Typically, this is the sort of approach used by a parent of a more skilled player. They sort of forget that for little Johnny to play second base all the time, someone else loses out on an opprtunity to play there.

TEE BALL TO-A-TEE

™

TeeBall Player Rotation System

Here's a workable plan of how to effectively (and fairly) rotate your players, keep order on the field, and happiness in the dugout and the stands.

HOW DO YOU <u>DO</u> THAT??!!??

One of the most difficult aspects of coaching a TeeBall team is figuring out a system of moving your players around equitably.

It can be a real struggle to find just the right mix of players to field the lineup in such a way that you are maximizing your players' strengths and minimizing their weaknesses. As coach, you are responsible for instructing your players during practice so that they can perform during games. You also owe it to your players to make this a positive learning experience. As such, no player should spend the majority of the season in the same position. While there will certainly be some players that will see more infield action than others because of a higher skill level, **NO PLAYER SHOULD BE "RELEGATED" EXCLUSIVELY TO THE OUTFIELD.**

Is that inflexible? No, not if you're trying to put the players' best interests first. Simply put, as coach it is incumbent upon you to field your team in such a way as to utilize your whole team. In TeeBall, this should be very simple. **ROTATE YOUR PLAYERS.** You will enjoy it more, the parents will enjoy it more, and the players will enjoy it more. (Certainly some kids are going to want to play the infield all the time, but you must explain to them that good ball players know how to play several positions. You might even list several current star players that play in the outfield.)

The best way to compose your fielding position is to teach each player at least one infield position and how to play the outfield properly. Even the most uncoordinated of players can be taught to stop the ball and tag the runner going to third or to throw the ball to first base. A good rule of thumb is to teach them an outfield position that corresponds to their infield position with simple instructions to follow if the ball is hit to them. In other words, if a youngster plays second base when in the infield, have them play a position in the outfield where if the ball is hit to them they are instructed to throw the ball to the second baseman. It's a good idea to teach right and right center fielders to throw the ball to second (with shortstop covering second base), and left and left centerfielders to throw the ball to shortstop (with second baseman covering second base). In most leagues, play is stopped once the ball is under control in the infield. Adjust your strategy for your league rules.

There are those who suggest that players are simply rotated from position to position in a numerical system.   (i.e. positions are assigned a numerical order and players are rotated by number, strictly 1 through 14. It could conceivably take two or three games for a player to find his/her way into the infield and conversely two or three games to find his/her way into the outfield.) A better way is to have a pattern set up whereby a player knows where he will go the next inning based on where was the prior inning.

BY WAY OF EXAMPLE:

Let's look at the players on the field represented by the numbers on the chart below. Let's assume for this example the team has 14 players. Most TeeBall teams have 12 - 14 players per team. They are numbered here for easy identification purposes ONLY:

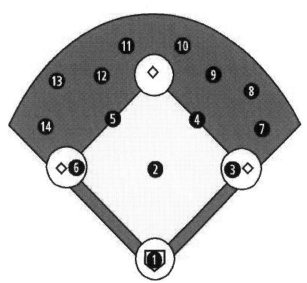

① **Catcher** - Most kids like to play catcher because they handle the ball a lot. Generally, this player will be one of your less skilled players. Use the opportunity to build throwing skills with this player. Rotate this player with positions 1$ and ι (the two corners of the outfield). Teach 14 to throw to short and 7 to throw to second base.

② **Pitcher** - Usually pitcher tends to be one of your better fielders - quick, sure hands and accurate throwing arm. Rotate this player into positions 1) or 1! in the outfield with instructions for them to field the ball quickly and either throw it to the person covering second in the event of a runner advancing to second, or move quickly (if they are within a few steps) to step on the base themselves to force the runner out.

③   **First Baseman** - First basemen generally catch the ball well. Rotate this player into position i in the outfield with instructions to back up the second baseman or players u or o in the outfield.

Tee Ball Player Rotation System

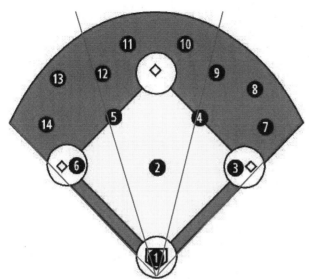

④ **Second Baseman** - As you will observe, an awful lot of balls tend to be hit to the right side of the infield. Most young players simply don't swing at the correct rate or angle to fully "get around on the ball" and tend to hit it to the right side. As a rule, next to your pitcher and first baseman, second base will get most of the infield plays. When rotating into the outfield, rotate into position o or 1) with instructions to back up player i or 1) (they can also be instructed to back up the second baseman in the event you have to put a less skilled player at position i or 1! in the outfield.

⑤   **Shortstop** - Shortstop, along with pitcher, first baseman and second baseman usually have the best glove on your team. When rotating this player into the outfield, move him/her into position 1@ or 1# with instructions to back up either the shortstop or the other player beside them.

By using this format, you should cover every position adequately while rotating the players in a logical way that makes it easy for them to understand what they should do. If you have 13 or 14 players on a team, there may be some games where some players get into the infield less than others. Keep track of how this balances out, making sure that you put the players who play in the infield fewer times in one game, receive more infield time the next game (It is a good idea to verbailze this plan to your parents too).

Additionally, it is a good idea to "stagger" your players in the outfield, zig-zagging one a few feet in front of the other in an alternating fashion. This keeps them from "bunching up" and makes it easier to stress that they should **ONLY GO AFTER A BALL HIT IN THEIR AREA.** (We've all seen the TeeBall games where the right fielder runs into left field to get a ball hit there). You might even divide the outfield into quadrants (see red lines dividing diagram above) specifying which area they are responsible for covering.

TEE BALL TO-A-TEE

FORMS TO MAKE YOUR TEEBALL COACHING LIFE EASIER

Oranizing your TeeBall practices and games just got easier! Here's a selection of forms created just for TeeBall coaches.

Forms To Make Your Tee Ball Coaching Life Easier

DISORGANIZED? HERE ARE FORMS TO HELP!

It really helps make the job of coaching a team easier to have a plan in place to use before practice and games. On the following pages you will find several forms which will make your job as coach much easier. By taking some time before each practice or game to organize your thoughts, prioritize your objectives, and put your practice or game plan on paper, you will maximize your success and minimize your stress.

Here are the forms on the following pages:

1.   **Practice Plan.1** - Included is a practice plan utilizing practice drills and skill-building exercises outlined in the **"Practice In A Pocket©" System** booklet.
     You can order the booklet by visiting *www.teeball-to-a-tee.com* on the web and clicking on the **"ORDER NOW"** link.

2.   **Practice Plan.2** - This version is blank for you to print and fill in yourself.

3.   **Batting Order** - This is a simple batting order form with 15 spaces for player names and numbers.

4.   **Field Rotation Plan.1** - This format is set up for vertical (portrait) use in your coaching notebook. It also includes spaces for batting order, making it a convenient one-sheet form for game use.

5.   **Field Rotation Plan.2** - This format is set up for horizontal (landscape) use in your coaching notebook. It also includes spaces for batting order, making it a convenient one-sheet form for game use.

Forms To Make Your Tee Ball Coaching Life Easier

PRACTICE PLAN.1

Here is a sample practice plan utilizing drills from the Clips 'N Tips© System. (This set of easy-to-use practice drills is part of this package you ordered.) We assume you will have a one-hour practice. Adjust accordingly for longer or shorter time availability. Length of drills should be approximately 5-10 minutes each. Run these drills simultaneously in different "stations" around the field. In most instances, you will only be able to successfully utilize 5-6 srills per practice. You can adjust your selections based upon the ability your players demonstrate while executing the drills. You may eliminate or add drills as required.

PRACTICE PLAN	(Put player initials in boxes above areas to be used for writing in number of repetitions of each drill. Use check boxes to indicate you did this drill.)											
Drill Player Initials *												
☐ Bounce It To The Bucket												
☐ Have A Catch With A Coach												
☐ "No Dropsies" Contest												
☐ Catching Flies												
☐ Who Can Catch The Coach?												
☐ Home to 2nd/2nd to Home Relay												
☐ Crab Drill												
☐ Crow Hop												
☐ Action-Distraction-Reaction												
☐ Stretching The Play												
☐ Just Block It												
☐ One And Two Pointers												
☐ Run Down But Not Out												
☐ Scoop-Up And Throw												
☐ To First Base And Beyond												
☐ "Bulls-Eye" Drill												
☐ Hit For Distance Drill												
☐ GO! or NO! Drill												
☐ Catching Fly Balls Drill												
☐ Advancing Baserunners On Hit Balls												
☐ "No Swarm" Outfield												
☐ Fielding Balls Hit to Outfield												
☐ Running To First Base Drill												
☐ Rounding The Bases Drill												
☐ Point To Da Man												
☐ Hip-Plosion Batting Drill												
☐ Fielding FUN-damentals												
☐ Fielding Bouncing Ground Balls												
☐ Moving Ground Balls												
☐ "Bulls-Eye" Wall Toss Drill												
☐ "Under & Over" Catching Drill												

www.teeball-to-a-tee.com

Forms To Make Your Tee Ball Coaching Life Easier

PRACTICE PLAN.2

Here is a practice form you can fill out for yourself. You can find an excellent beginning practice format in the section of this handbook entitled, "A Great Beginning Tee Ball Practice Routine".

Remember: Keep practices moving and have a sense of enjoyment and excitement about what you are doing - the kids will also!

PRACTICE PLAN	(Put player initials in boxes above areas to be used for writing in number of repetitions of each drill. Use check boxes to indicate you did this drill.)													
Drill Player Initials *														
☐														
☐														
☐														
☐														
☐														
☐														
☐														
☐														
☐														
☐														
☐														
☐														
☐														
☐														
☐														
☐														
☐														
☐														
☐														
☐														
☐														
☐														
☐														
☐														
☐														
☐														
☐														
☐														

BATTING ORDER

Copy this page and trim as needed to create a batting order for your team.

Forms To Make Your Tee Ball Coaching Life Easier

FIELD ROTATION PLANS 1 & 2

The following pages present two formats of a field rotation form for your use. Use whichever form best suits the way you work in your coaches' notebook. Copy or print out these pages as needed to create a workable rotation plan for your team.

There are spaces at each position for up to 14 players. If you need to add additional players, simply write their name in any blank spaces.

It is suggested that you keep a copy of where your players have played in previous games in your notebook so you can easily keep track of how you are rotating players. You can also show this to any parent who needs some assurance that you are trying to do this in a fair and equitable manner.

As a further suggestion, it is recommended to keep 2-3 "stronger" players in the infield during any given rotation. This gives you at least a few players that you feel sure can catch the ball to make a play. This will heighten everyone's confidence and enjoyment. Rotate these players out the next inning and replace with 2-3 more skilled players. If you put all of your best players in the infield at once, be prepared to rotate them all at once if need be. See the section on **"Tee Ball Players Rotation System"** for recommended rotation strategy.

Remember: These are not inflexible rules. They are simply recommended suggestions which have been proven to work!

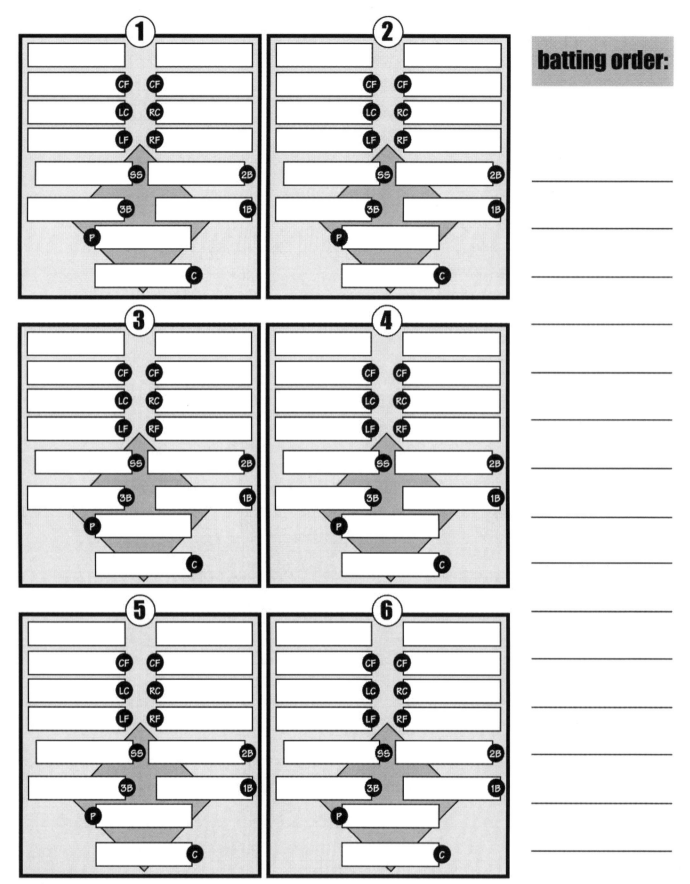

batting order:

_____

_____

_____

_____

_____

_____

_____

_____

_____

_____

_____

_____

NOTES:

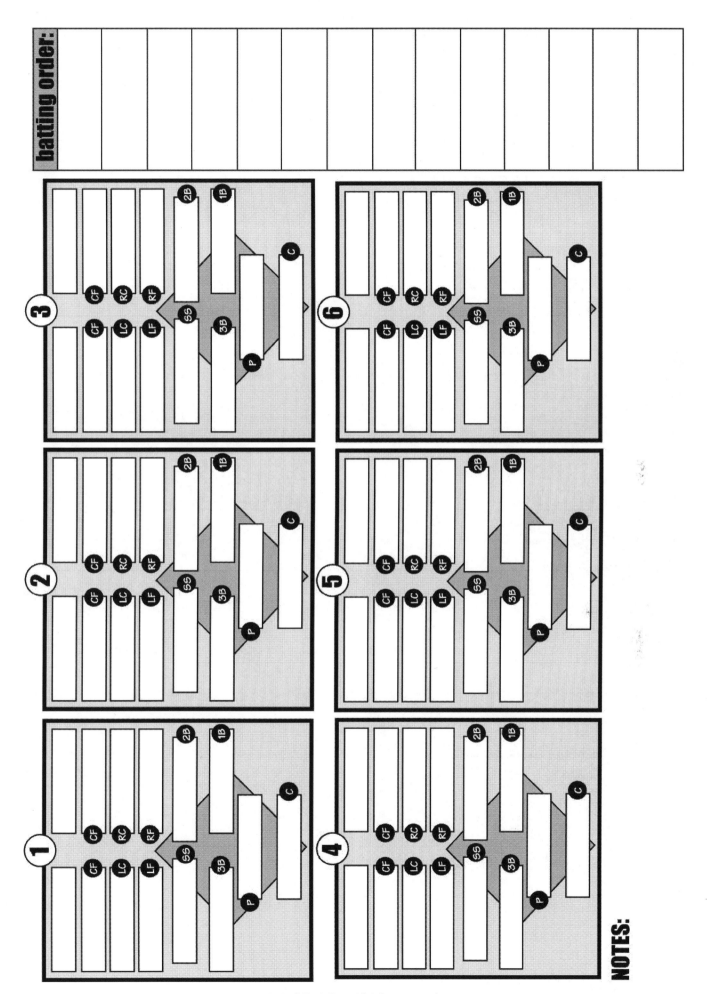

batting order:

NOTES:

TEE BALL TO-A-TEE

AWARDS, Incentives, and Motivational Helpers

Here's a selection of easy-to-use awards and motivational handouts to help spur your team on to greater success while recognizing their accomplishments

EVERYBODY LOVES RECOGNITION.

Everybody. Kids. Parents. Coaches. <u>Everybody.</u>

People love to get patted on the backs, and people love to see others get recognition for a job well done. Especially if those people are parents and the others getting the recognition are their children.

Sometimes as a coach it is difficult to cover all the demands of coaching while attending to the countless other details as well. This section of your Coaching Handbook will make you a **SUPER-STAR** in your own right.

We've done the hard part - creating the artwork for the specific awards. You simply print out as many copies of the following awards and motivational helpers as you need on your printer, fill in the appropriate blanks, hand them out to the appropriate individuals, and **PRESTO - INSTANT RECOGNITION!**

✪ BIG-TIME IMPORTANT COACHING TIP ✪

Keep a record of any awards that you give over the course of the season. It is especially important in TeeBall that you distribute praise and awards fairly equitably. Use your imagination (and these awards and motivators) and you'll be able to give recognition to the truly deserving as well as the struggling player who needs a boost.

✪ BIG-TIME IMPORTANT COACHING TIP #2 ✪

While you're at it - you can never give too many awards in TeeBall. Giving a game ball to a player (or two - keep a couple extra going during the game) is a great motivator for the players.

TeeBall Superstar

Offensive Player of the Game

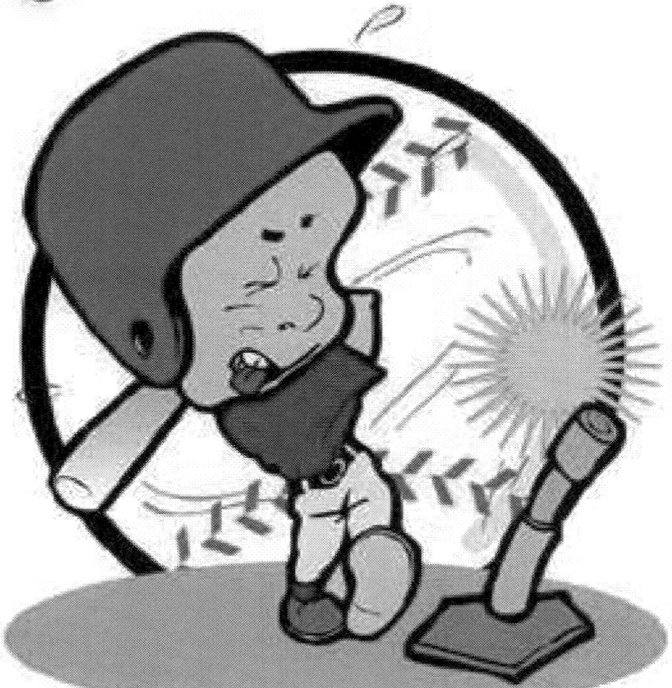

This is to certify that

____

Player Name

played an incredible game displaying awesome offensive power to help his team on

____

Game Date

while playing for

____

Team Name

____

Coach Signature

 www.teeball-to-a-tee.com

Tee Ball To-A-Tee

TEEBALL

DEFENSIVE

Defensive Player
of the Game

This is to certify that

_____
Player Name

played an awesome game displaying exceptional defensive skills
to help his team on

_____
Game Date

while playing for

_____
Team Name

_____
Coach Signature

TEEBALL I Made The Play of the Day!

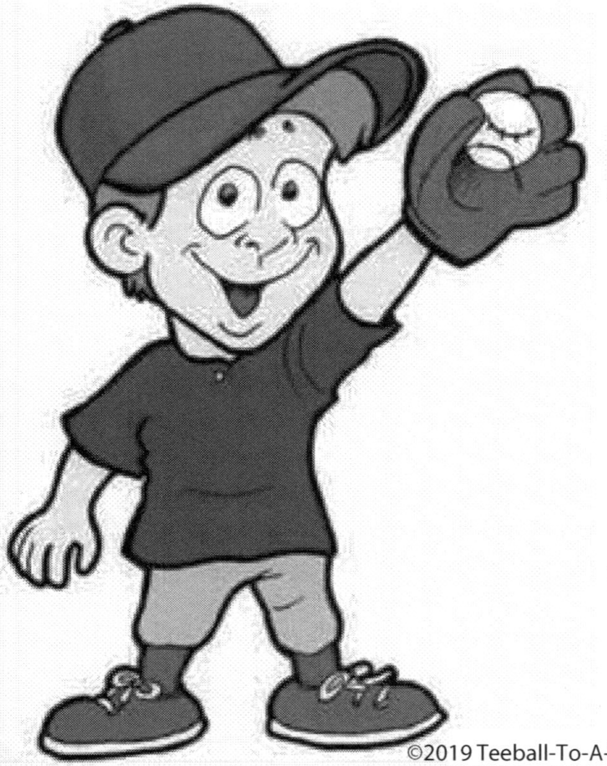

This is to certify that

____

Player Name

made the OUTSTANDING PLAY OF THE DAY
to help his team on

____

Game Date

while playing for

____

Team Name

____

Coach Signature

www.teeball-to-a-tee.com

TEEBALL AWARD

This is to certify that

_____
Player Name

**displayed OUTSTANDING HUSTLE
to help his team on**

_____
Game Date

while playing for

_____
Team Name

_____
Coach Signature

©2019 Teeball-To-A-Tee   www.teeball-to-a-tee.com

LISTENING TO DA TEE BALL COACH!

This is to certify that

_____
Player Name

did an excellent job of LISTENING TO THE COACH
to help his team on

_____
Game Date

while playing for

_____
Team Name

_____
Coach Signature

©2019 Teeball-To-A-Tee

www.teeball-to-a-tee.com

TEE BALL TO-A-TEE™

YOU Can Be A Super Coach!

Sure-fire ways you can be an effective coach and a Hero to kids and parents alike!

GET READY TO ADJUST YOUR CAPE.

Your kids and parents will almost expect you to stop a train with your bare hands.

Seriously, you will become your teams' hero just by virtue of being their coach. If you do a good job, teach them something and have fun - well, you will make even Superman look wimpy.

Your players and their parents **WANT** to like their coach. They **WANT** to feel that their child has learned something about the game. They **WANT** to see improvement in their child's basic baseball skills. They **WANT** their child to enjoy a positive sports experience.

By implementing the ideas presented in this Coaching Handbook, you will go a long way towards helping them achieve those goals. Additionally, **YOU** will feel very good about what you have done. **YOU** will have a great season and enjoy the relationships you start with young players and their families. **YOU** will enjoy the incomparable feeling that comes only from that special moment when you overhear one of your players introduce you to one of their buddies as **"COACH."**

Most of all, **YOU** will get tremendous satisfaction and enjoyment out of the time you spend with your own child. The time that you spend practicing, "having a catch," and just having fun will be great bonding time with your child that cannot be measured by trophies or awards. **YOU** will cherish these memories for a lifetime.

Before we close, here's a last minute checklist of

A DOZEN QUICK TIPS FOR BEING A "SUPER COACH"

1. Get to practice early and expect that your players arrive on time.
2. Share responsibilities with another coach or other helpers. This will give players more individual attention and help keep them active and involved.
3. Keep activities and drills brief (5-10 minutes each).
4. Provide as many contacts with the ball as possible - throwing, catching, fielding and hitting. In a game, players may only get four or five chances (at most) to field a ball. They must get many more contacts in practice to improve.
5. Do the more demanding skills and drills early in the practice.
6. Challenge players by increasing the difficulty of drills once they have mastered easier ones.
7. Treat all players equally and emphasize positive feedback. Try to talk to every player indivudually at every practice.

Make sure you include the following elements in every practice:

8. **WARM UP** - Easy run or warm up activity followed by stretching.
9. **THROWING AND CATCHING** - Spend time each practice developing throwing form, accuracy, and arm strength.
10. **DEFENSIVE SKILLS** - Practice all defensive skills used in a game on a regular basis.
11. **BATTING PRACTICE** - Use stations in order to cover batting practice effectively while ensuring all other aspects of practice are covered.
12. **BASE RUNNING** - Use races and relays to improve running technique. Some elements of base running can be incorporated into batting practice.

TEE BALL TO-A-TEE ™

BUT WAIT, WHAT HAVE WE LEARNED?

Review what you've learned and what you can hope for from your players (and yourself) in the future.

You Mean We Learned All <u>That</u>?

After going thorugh this process, what have you learned - what have you **REALLY** learned?

If you're like most of the folks we've heard from who have used the TeeBall-To-A-Tee materials, quite a bit! The single-most recurring theme we've heard in our e-mail testimonials and letters has been this: **"I learned to keep coaching in perspective."** That's it. Not, "I learned a great new drill that enabled my kids to all hit home runs," or "Every kid was so focused and attentive during the drills," or even, "My team's parents all think I am the Best. Coach. Ever."

While we've gotten plenty of e-mails that tout the training methods we present here, and we get lots of praise for the drills, awards, and games we talk about, we're most proud of the **ATTITUDE** that most of the coaches are now exhibiting. We've had many coaches tell us that our methods have helped them enjoy coaching their own children more than ever before.

Simply put, most folks come away from the experience feeling that they've done much more than build a better young ballplayer or construct a better team. Most of what we hear is that something really special has happened in their relationship with their own kid(s) as well as the kids of others. Many have reported even seeing a change in even the most difficult parents once they've gone through the season.

As an addendum to this Handbook, we have put together some of the most valuable things that you and the players on your team will learn during your season together. You'll find that the experience when handled properly will be a worthwhile learning experience for you, your team, and the parents and extended families. You might find it hard to believe that coaching a teeball team could be a valuable learning experience for you and benefits would be tangible and intangible, but it's true. You might even be thinking, *"I didn't want to <u>learn</u> anything - I just thought i would be fun to coach my daughter's teeball team."*

KNOW THIS: The things you learn in coaching a teeball team might very well be so valuable that you might find yourself applying the same principles to those with whom you work and your family at home. Seriously.

How, you say? Read on and discover ...

EVERYTHING I NEED TO KNOW IN LIFE, I LEARNED IN TEEBALL

There are some interesting theories out there about how we learn and what we learn. But nothing is more certain than this: Whenever we **experience** something, we **learn** something - whether we realize it or not. In the case of coaching a teeball team, you have the rare opportunity to influence whether the learning experience is a positive or a negative one. **Most** of us would like to think that when the kids grow up and they recall their first coach **(YOU)**, they'll say it fondly and remember what a great experience it was, and **NOT** be wondering where you live and if they could get enough eggs to do justice to your house.

Here are some of the skills **YOU, YOUR PLAYERS, and THEIR FAMILIES** will learn in the course of your season together:

REALISTIC EXPECTATIONS:
While you may succeed in teaching your players how to do amazing things, it is best to not let your expectations outstrip their capabilities. Simply put, a team of 4 and 5-year-olds is not always going to perform like a precision machine. Quite frankly, more often than not, they are going to operate more like something dreamed up by, well, a group of 4 and 5-year-olds. Expect them to do great things - after all, you're their coach and you need to expect them to do their best. But if their best on any given day is playing in the dirt, watching airplanes fly overhead, or collecting bugs in their cap - well, so be it. On another day, they will surprise you with their focus and determination. *This is a fun game and I like to play.*

COMMUNICATION:
Few things can be more elementary than trying to explain a basic skill to a kid that has no framce of reference for the skill at all. If a kid doesn't know where left field is for example, how can he/she go there, unless you tell them? If you don't communicate to a young player that he has to touch first base before he runs to second after hitting a double, how will he know? If you don't properly demonstrate the correct way to catch a fly ball, how in the world would a 4 or 5-year old know? In short, you will learn the valuable skill of clear communication with your team. You will understand the real virture of presenting information in short, easy-to-digest chunks of information. *I understand - and I believe I can do it.*

LEARNING - NOT MEMORIZING:
All of us has certain information that we retain **all our lives.** There's some thing(s) that you had to learn in school that you've simply remembered ever since. You may have memorized it, but in reality you **learned** it. It was **taught** to you, by someone who realized the value of truly learning it versus simple memorization. All of us can speak to having memorized something long enough to pass a test, with the information never to cross our conscious mind again. Similarly, we can all testify to learning something that is so indelibly imprinted in our minds that cannot recall ever not knowing it. It will be that way with the skills you teach your players - they will build on them, enhance them, refine them, or whatever - but the **teaching** you did will stay with them forever. *I know how to do it - let me do it.*

FINDING THE SKILL THAT PROMOTES SUCCESS RATHER THAN FAILURE:
Some people knock teeball because they feel like it doesn't celebrate real achievement because every player bats, every kid (should) play the infield, etc. They feel that this causes a "watering-down" process in sports because "everybody plays." I encourage coaches to find that one (or more) skill or ability that you can develop in every young player to help them be a contributor to the team's success. Even the player you feel can't possibly help your team can contribute in some special way - as a coach, it is your responsibility to find it. *I am good at this - watch me do it.*

INSTILLING A DESIRE TO SUCCEED ON MULTIPLE LEVELS:
By doing this to your team, you will also do it to yourself. I have always told my players that "if one area of your game is not your strength, work on another area and contribute in that way. That will help you get better in all areas of your game." What that means is this: if a player struggles in hitting, help them develop defensive skills that will make them a better overall player. We've all seen the young player that strikes out (again) that slumps dejectedly and shuffles to his position in the field only to miss the ball when it's hit to him on the very next play. Helping that player be ready and able to make the defensive play can give them the **confidence** (see next item) to work harder to improve their hitting, or baserunning, or any number of other skills. *I can do <u>this</u> well - and I want to learn how to do <u>that</u> too.*

BUILD CONFIDENCE:
Most of us have had a boss that we have liked. Often, whether we realize it or not, we like them because of the way they make us feel about ourselves. If you've had a boss that has made you feel like you've done a good job, chances are pretty good you have a high opinion of that person. That's **not** to say you should congratulate someone who does a poor job, or even say something positive that you don't mean,

it **does** mean you should look for the positive and use it to build upon. You can generally always find something positive a kid has done during the course of the game to praise them for. "Jeff - you did a great job of backing up Timmy on those balls hit into the outfield today- just like in practice." Even if Jeff simply did a marginal job today, chances are pretty good he will do a better job next game. ***If you believe I can do this - I believe I can too.***

BRING OUT THE BEST.

In them, in you, and in their parents. So, how do you do this? By setting an example - in the way you coach, the way you think and the way you behave. We all hear the stories of coaches whose bad examples of preferential coaching treatment, poor sportsmanship, and negative attitudes seem to hold sway on youth sports.

But it doesn't have to be that way. You **CAN** be the coach who sets a positive example in these and other areas. What's more you can lead by example, showing the way for other coaches to see your positive demeanor and honorable character as a yardstick for themselves, perhaps. Certainly, if nothing else, you can be the example for your team's players, parents and "extended family."

If your players see you as a coach they can trust - who conducts himself honorably, and treats the team fairly, they will respond to you better in the long haul. What's more, they will move on from your team and carry some of those attributes to their next team and allow them to develop their own sense of fair play and "best behavior." This works for parents as well. Even those parents who tend to behave poorly during a game will temper their behavior if they observe that you keep yourself under control. Even if they don't change their behavior long term, they will generally be motivated to "tone it down" by the "buying in" to your plan by the rest of the parents. ***I'm going to play fair because my coach does.***

TEAM BUILDING.

By working hard to develop all the palyers on your team, rather than a select few, you will be promoting a real sense of the "Team Concept." Once I played a coach (who was the coach of the team considered the "best" by a consensus of the other coaches) during the end of the season tournament who during the pre-game chat confided how he was going to play the game against us. Essentially, his "star players" in the infield were going to hold us to few or no runs by not allowing us to score any runs. They were going to score the maximum allowable number of runs for two innings to build a comfortable lead - and **THEN** he was going to put his "weaker kids" (his words not mine - they had played in the outfield all season) in the infield for an inning before the game was called. I was furious - he discussed the whole thing as if our kids weren't even there - completely discounting our ability to compete. I told my other coaches what he said, but not the kids.

It looked like his plan was a pretty good one because they batted first and scored seven runs while we nervously made several errors, hurting ourselves. Making matters worse, we didn't score any runs in the bottom of the inning. But after our kids got over the their jitters of playing "the best team," they settled down and played much better. They didn't make any more errors and completely shut the other team's offense down - allowing no more runs to be scored! Our team scored the maximum over the next two innings piling up 22 runs! The other coach even moved his "star players" to the outfield early in an attempt to stop us from scoring.
He had them playing back against the fence simply to stop the ball and throw it in. Of course the poor kids he moved into the infield had no idea what to do and struggled as they had very few opportunities to play in the infield during the course of the season *(Oddly enough, they received the brunt of his post-game criticism).*

The secret? While I wish it was some "Knute Rockne" - type speech I had given them, I think it was all kid-driven. The kids all believed in themselves and they supported each other, and believed they could play better. Because we had moved players around during the season, they all knew what they should do and what was expected of each other. Once they recovered from their nervousness, they started playing better and started having fun. They realized that they **could** play with the other guys, and simply did what kids do when given the opportunity - they played their best -- as a **TEAM.**
I will do the best job I can wherever I am for my <u>team</u>.

LAYING THE FOUNDATION.
Essentially, all of the things we have discussed in this "Coaches' Handbook" point to one ultimate goal: **"Laying the Foundation."** If by some chance, you motivate some child to believe in himself and encourage him to participate in the sport if for no other reason than to enjoy the game as a knowledgeable fan, you've achieved a worthy goal. Not every kid goes on to play travel ball, high school , college or pro ball (most don't). Some quit along the way, driven out of the game by coaches, parents, or their peers. Some quit because they realize they want to play something else, or just simply develop other interests. But **SOME**, continue to play rec league ball just for the pleasure of it, as long as there is a league in which to play.
It is for those players, we should strive to be the Best Coach We Can Be.
I will play baseball because it's fun, and because I like the game.

CLIPS 'N TIPS

FOR TEE BALL PLAYERS

WAYS TO MAKE PRACTICE AND GAMES MORE FUN AND PROVIDE A BETTER LEARNING EXPERIENCE FOR PLAYERS, COACHES & FAMILIES.

The unique **"Clips 'N Tips" System**© features coaching, training and practice planning tips for parents and coaches as they work with young ballplayers to help them develop their game. This handy Coach's Clipboard Guide will assist the Parent/Coach in planning their team's season from the very first day of "Spring Training" through the season's end.

Keep your Clipboard handy at every practice for finding the perfect drill or during the games to update and evaluate your players' progress.

CONTENTS

EVERYBODY'S GOTTA START SOMEWHERE!

TWO MAJOR QUESTIONS most parent/coaches have regarding tee ball is, "How in the world did I get myself talked into coaching a group of hyperactive 4, 5 & 6 - year olds on how to play baseball?" and "Where do I begin?"

CHANCES ARE you volunteered because you thought it would be fun to spend that one-on-one time with your son or daughter, and maybe, just maybe, you could do a pretty good job. Well, you are going to coach your child's team (**CONGRATULATIONS!**), and now you're wondering, "What next?"

If your league is like most youth leagues in the Tee Ball division, you've got a lot of kids interested in playing, and most leagues will have 13 or 14 kids per team. WOW! You may be saying by now, "How do I handle that many kids? How do I teach anybody anything! How will I even survive the season?!?"

Well, it can be done and one tool you can use to make it all happen is the one you're holding in your hands.

The Clips 'N Tips System© will give you solid ideas to help you:
1.) **REALIZE** what skill level your players have,
2.) **ORGANIZE** a developmental practice and skill-building program,
3.) **PRIORITIZE** what skills and fudamentals you need to develop,
4.) **MAXIMIZE** Practice time!

HAVE FUN!

KEYS TO COACHING TEE BALL PLAYERS

Going to a first Tee ball practice session can be a little overwhelming for players and parents alike. Kids are a little nervous and hopeful they will do well and have fun. Parents are usually concerned with whether or not their child's coach will be a taskmaster or a teacher. Coaches can go a long way to ensuring a successful season by making each practice and game an exercise in encouragement. Each child should have an opportunity to succeed within the parameters of their particular skill level.

SERVE 'EM A SANDWICH

Success must be measured in terms that can easily be grasped by the youngest of players. "Great job Jason! You almost made it to first base! Next time, make sure you run all the way past first like we did in practice. Way to hit the ball!" is much better than, "Come on Jason! Why didn't you run hard to first!?!"

Successes — throwing the ball in the general direction of first base, hitting the ball off the tee, being in the "ready position" — should all be noticed and praised by the coach(es). Sandwich instruction between genuine praises to have the maximum positive impact. Small praises add up to build confidence and skills. Concentrate on what they learned today.

BE YOUR TEAM'S "COACH"

Kids look up to their **"Coach."** **"Coach"** has a love for the sport. **"Coach"** has a love for the kids - and shows it. **"Coach"** must be patient, and have an ability to motivate positively.

10 QUICK TIPS TO A PERFECT PRACTICE!

1. Make your practices relatively short. Tee ballers (ages 4-6), in general, have shorter attention spans.

2. Organize practice so there's no downtime.
    Don't let kids stand around and watch - they need to perform the skill-building drills.

3. Enlist the help of lots of parents. This encourages participation and discourages complaining.

4. Explain and demonstrate what you expect before you begin a drill.
    They can't do it right unless you show them what you expect and will accept.

5. Break into small groups of four or five (or smaller!) when teaching new skills. This allows the players more "hands-on" time, making practice fun.

6. Vary the drills as they master the skills. This is important as they progress, and helps keep them from   getting bored.

7. Make "games" out of practice. Incorporate a reward system to instill the desire to succeed in a particular skill - such as fielding the ball cleanly. Keep track of each player's progress and declare the "Skill Champion Of The Day." Have one "Offensive Skill Champion" and one "Defensive Skill Champion" per practice. Make sure everyone is recognized at some point.

8. Simple rewards reap big benefits. A **GENUINE** positive word does wonders for a players' self-esteem.   They know when you're faking it - so point out something valid (ie: "Way to hustle, Kelsey! You almost beat the throw!")

9. Recap. Review what's been learned.

10. Encourage practice at home. Set up a couple of drills they can do at home with family or friends. Give handpouts if necessary - make copies of particular "Clips 'N Tips" drill sheets if they are struggling sith specific skills.

(REMEMBER, SIMPLICITY AND REPETITION ARE KEY!)

COACHING TEE BALL: SPECIFIC PRACTICE CHECKLIST

(MAKE SURE YOU DO THESE!)

- ☐ Contact All Players & Families
- ☐ Notify Them Of Practice Schedule
- ☐ Provide hard copy of Practice Schedule
- ☐ Provide Roster & Phone List to Families
- ☐ Organize Practice Routines (see pgs 31-34)
- ☐ Plan Drill List/Skill Breakdown (see pgs 35-46)
- ☐ Gather equipment/materials for practice
- ☐ Clips 'N Tips
- ☐ Batting Helmets
- ☐ Bats

- ☐ Bucket of tee balls/other soft balls
- ☐ Throw down bases
- ☐ Extra Gloves
- ☐ Tee (Very important in tee ball!)
- ☐ Plastic cones
- ☐ Coaches Notebook
- ☐ Player Rewards
- ☐ Player Bonus Forms
- ☐ Water Cooler/cups (on a hot day)

Other Important Things To Bring To Practice

- ☐ A great attitude
- ☐ A sense of humor
- ☐ A sense of perspective
- ☐ Enthusiasm
- ☐ Patience

TEACH THEM TO "BE READY"

What's one of the simplest things you can teach even the youngest player that will benefit them greatly? Teach them to "BE READY."

THE READY POSITION - Each infielder should pretend that every batter is going to attempt to hit a ground ball to him on every pitch. Then the infielder won't be surprised when the ball leaves the bat and heads in his direction. If the coach can get the younger player to play this mind game with himself on every pitch, then when the ball does come to him he will be ready to get in position to make the play.

A great method to get them focused (if only for the moment) is at the start of every defensive inning, the manager calls out, "Who's ready?". Those who are ready and focused respond by raising their hand or yelling back to the coach, "Ready!". Typically, all will respond positively at the beginning of the inning. You can also do this prior to every third or fourth batter to cue them back into the game if you see them "drifting."

This player has correctly assumed the "Ready Position."

TeeBall-To-A-Tee has compiled many effective drills for Tee Ballers.
It is important that practice activities also have fun content, given the ages and attention spans of the participants.
It is important that prior to starting any new drill or skill-building exercise, that it be demonstrated properly by a coach several times with a clear, easy-to-understand explanation.

THE BEST TEACHER IS PRACTICE, PRACTICE, PRACTICE.

The following pages offer several easy-to-remember drills applicable for all skill levels.

Have a clear idea which drills you will be working on at any given practice.
You should only copy and take with you to practice the pages you will either utilize in that practice, or include specific copies of drills for players to practice at home.
If you are fortunate to have plenty of assistant coaches or parents to assist with practice, you might want to give them each a sheet of drills to work on with their group.
Make sure they understand how to execute the drill properly before beginning to demonstrate to the players in their group.

"IF YOU DON'T KNOW WHERE
YOU'RE GOING,
YOU MIGHT NOT GET THERE."
- YOGI BERRA

Evaluating your players accurately and helping them develop as players is just as important to the development of your team as it is to the individual player. By evaluating each player properly and understanding their strengths and weaknesses, you can help them improve their skills and enhance their progress as they grow and move further along into organized youth baseball.

Baseball is a game whereby skills are developed through repetitive successful completion of various skill sets. Drills are are designed to promote and enhance muscle memory in the hope that as a player masters these skills he/she will perform the skill at a level consistent to what they have achieved through consistent practice.

By practicing the drills on the following pages, you will see your players improve over the course of your teeball season.

With some players, you will see that they already have a mastery of certain skill sets because of their athleticism, older siblings or involved parent/coaching. With others, you will find that you will have to focus on a few specific skill sets to improve their chances for improvement and success. Make sure that each player thoroughly understands the drill before attempting to execute the drill.

Frustration for coach and player alike is sure to result from improper explanation and demonstration of the drill(s).

The following pages contain **LOTS** of drills designed specifically for teeball players as well as forms to help you and your assistant coaches evaluate and track your players' progress during the course of your season.

Bounce It To The Bucket.
Put a large basket or cooler on a base. Outfielders try to throw and bounce the ball to hit the target. 10 points for getting the ball in, 5 for hitting the bucket and 1 point for the nearest bounce, no matter where the ball ends up. This drill teaches throwing from the outfield to a base.

Have A Catch With A Coach.
A player and a coach (or parent helper) play catch standing approximately ten feet apart. Focus on proper throwing technique. Make a game of it and keep score of the number of successful catches. This drill teaches proper throwing and catching technique.

PRACTICE PLAN

(Put player initials in boxes above areas to be used for writing in number of repetitions of each drill. Use check boxes to indicate you did this drill.)

Drill Player Initials *																
☐ Bounce It To The Bucket																
☐ Have A Catch With A Coach																
☐ "No Dropsies" Contest																
☐ Catching Flies																
☐ Who Can Catch The Coach?																
☐ Home to 2nd/2nd to Home Relay																
☐ Crab Drill																
☐ Crow Hop																
☐ Action-Distraction-Reaction																
☐ Stretching The Play																
☐ Just Block It																
☐ One And Two Pointers																
☐ Run Down But Not Out																
☐ Scoop-Up And Throw																
☐ To First Base And Beyond																
☐ "Bulls-Eye" Drill																
☐ Hit For Distance Drill																
☐ GO! or NO! Drill																
☐ Catching Fly Balls Drill																
☐ Advancing Baserunners On Hit Balls																
☐ "No Swarm" Outfield																
☐ Fielding Balls Hit to Outfield																
☐ Running To First Base Drill																
☐ Rounding The Bases Drill																
☐ Point To Da Man																
☐ Hip-Plosion Batting Drill																
☐ Fielding FUN-damentals																
☐ Fielding Bouncing Ground Balls																
☐ Moving Ground Balls																
☐ "Bulls-Eye" Wall Toss Drill																
☐ "Under & Over" Catching Drill																

"No Dropsies" Contest.
Players are in pairs and throw the ball back and forth between each other. If they drop a ball, their team is out. Last pair that has not dropped a ball wins. This drill teaches the players to focus on making the catch and holding onto the ball.

Catching Flies.
Hit or throw fly balls to fielders by using a soft baseball, rubber ball or tennis ball. Be sure to demonstrate the proper technique (ie: how to position the glove, how to cover the ball with the other hand, etc.). How many can they catch in a row? Repetition is the key to success. This drill teaches and reinforces proper fly ball catching techniques.

PRACTICE PLAN

(Put player initials in boxes above areas to be used for writing in number of repetitions of each drill. Use check boxes to indicate you did this drill.

Drill Player Initials *																
☐ Bounce It To The Bucket																
☐ Have A Catch With A Coach																
☐ "No Dropsies" Contest																
☐ Catching Flies																
☐ Who Can Catch The Coach?																
☐ Home to 2nd/2nd to Home Relay																
☐ Crab Drill																
☐ Crow Hop																
☐ Action-Distraction-Reaction																
☐ Stretching The Play																
☐ Just Block It																
☐ One And Two Pointers																
☐ Run Down But Not Out																
☐ Scoop-Up And Throw																
☐ To First Base And Beyond																
☐ "Bulls-Eye" Drill																
☐ Hit For Distance Drill																
☐ GO! or NO! Drill																
☐ Catching Fly Balls Drill																
☐ Advancing Baserunners On Hit Balls																
☐ "No Swarm" Outfield																
☐ Fielding Balls Hit to Outfield																
☐ Running To First Base Drill																
☐ Rounding The Bases Drill																
☐ Point To Da Man																
☐ Hip-Plosion Batting Drill																
☐ Fielding FUN-damentals																
☐ Fielding Bouncing Ground Balls																
☐ Moving Ground Balls																
☐ "Bulls-Eye" Wall Toss Drill																
☐ "Under & Over" Catching Drill																

Who Can Catch the Coach?

Coach runs from home plate to first base. After a few steps, coach shouts "tag me" to a player holding a ball, who runs after the coach and tries to tag him out. Coach to decide where/when/if the player attempting the tag is successful. This skill teaches pursuit until the tag is made.

Home to Second/Second to Home Relay.

Coach puts half the team at home plate, the other half at second base. At the command "GO!" first player at each position runs to the other position (ie: home to second; second to home). Once the player has arrived at the next position, the next player on his team runs to the next position. This drill is continued until all players have run once. This skill develops baserunning speed.

PRACTICE PLAN

(Put player initials in boxes above areas to be used for writing in number of repetitions of each drill. Use check boxes to indicate you did this drill.)

Drill Player Initials *														
☐ Bounce It To The Bucket														
☐ Have A Catch With A Coach														
☐ "No Dropsies" Contest														
☐ Catching Flies														
☐ Who Can Catch The Coach?														
☐ Home to 2nd/2nd to Home Relay														
☐ Crab Drill														
☐ Crow Hop														
☐ Action-Distraction-Reaction														
☐ Stretching The Play														
☐ Just Block It														
☐ One And Two Pointers														
☐ Run Down But Not Out														
☐ Scoop-Up And Throw														
☐ To First Base And Beyond														
☐ "Bulls-Eye" Drill														
☐ Hit For Distance Drill														
☐ GO! or NO! Drill														
☐ Catching Fly Balls Drill														
☐ Advancing Baserunners On Hit Balls														
☐ "No Swarm" Outfield														
☐ Fielding Balls Hit to Outfield														
☐ Running To First Base Drill														
☐ Rounding The Bases Drill														
☐ Point To Da Man														
☐ Hip-Plosion Batting Drill														
☐ Fielding FUN-damentals														
☐ Fielding Bouncing Ground Balls														
☐ Moving Ground Balls														
☐ "Bulls-Eye" Wall Toss Drill														
☐ "Under & Over" Catching Drill														

Crab Drill.

Player is in basic fielding position stance - crouched forward with glove open and down. Player steps to the ball as the coach rolls the ball for them to field. Vary this by rolling the ball to one side or another, teaching them to move laterally. This drill reinforces proper fielding position and correct technique in fielding balls which move to either side of the player. (Increase the difficulty of the play attempt as the season progresses and the player improves.)

Crow Hop.

Player takes a short step and a hop in the direction of the throw ending with the index finger pointing toward the intended target. The coach (or parent helper) throws the ball to the player, and the player throws the ball back using this method. This drill teaches proper body mechanics on the throw.

PRACTICE PLAN

(Put player initials in boxes above areas to be used for writing in number of repetitions of each drill. Use check boxes to indicate you did this drill.

Drill Player Initials *													
☐ Bounce It To The Bucket													
☐ Have A Catch With A Coach													
☐ "No Dropsies" Contest													
☐ Catching Flies													
☐ Who Can Catch The Coach?													
☐ Home to 2nd/2nd to Home Relay													
☐ Crab Drill													
☐ Crow Hop													
☐ Action-Distraction-Reaction													
☐ Stretching The Play													
☐ Just Block It													
☐ One And Two Pointers													
☐ Run Down But Not Out													
☐ Scoop-Up And Throw													
☐ To First Base And Beyond													
☐ "Bulls-Eye" Drill													
☐ Hit For Distance Drill													
☐ GO! or NO! Drill													
☐ Catching Fly Balls Drill													
☐ Advancing Baserunners On Hit Balls													
☐ "No Swarm" Outfield													
☐ Fielding Balls Hit to Outfield													
☐ Running To First Base Drill													
☐ Rounding The Bases Drill													
☐ Point To Da Man													
☐ Hip-Plosion Batting Drill													
☐ Fielding FUN-damentals													
☐ Fielding Bouncing Ground Balls													
☐ Moving Ground Balls													
☐ "Bulls-Eye" Wall Toss Drill													
☐ "Under & Over" Catching Drill													

Action - Distraction - Reaction.
Coach rolls the ball to a fielder, but another player runs in front of the fielder and tries to break the fielder's concentration on catching the ball. If the player successfully fields the ball, he is awarded a point. The player with the most points at the end of this drill wins. This drill reinforces the importance of being focused on the ball and blocking out distractions.

Stretching The Play.
Coach throws or hits ball to one side or the other of a fielder, far enough that he/she has to "stretch" (or move laterally) to field the ball. Then, the fielder must throw to first base. This drill teaches a player to "go after" a ball outside the "easy play zone" and make the follow-up play.

PRACTICE PLAN

(Put player initials in boxes above areas to be used for writing in number of repetitions of each drill. Use check boxes to indicate you did this drill.

Drill — Player Initials *															
☐ Bounce It To The Bucket															
☐ Have A Catch With A Coach															
☐ "No Dropsies" Contest															
☐ Catching Flies															
☐ Who Can Catch The Coach?															
☐ Home to 2nd/2nd to Home Relay															
☐ Crab Drill															
☐ Crow Hop															
☐ Action-Distraction-Reaction															
☐ Stretching The Play															
☐ Just Block It															
☐ One And Two Pointers															
☐ Run Down But Not Out															
☐ Scoop-Up And Throw															
☐ To First Base And Beyond															
☐ "Bulls-Eye" Drill															
☐ Hit For Distance Drill															
☐ GO! or NO! Drill															
☐ Catching Fly Balls Drill															
☐ Advancing Baserunners On Hit Balls															
☐ "No Swarm" Outfield															
☐ Fielding Balls Hit to Outfield															
☐ Running To First Base Drill															
☐ Rounding The Bases Drill															
☐ Point To Da Man															
☐ Hip-Plosion Batting Drill															
☐ Fielding FUN-damentals															
☐ Fielding Bouncing Ground Balls															
☐ Moving Ground Balls															
☐ "Bulls-Eye" Wall Toss Drill															
☐ "Under & Over" Catching Drill															

Just Block It.
Coach hits ball directly to a fielder. Emphasis is on stopping the ball to keep it from getting through to the outfield. It is OK to just block the ball. This drill can be a game with a point scored for every block, two for a catch and zero if the ball is not stopped. This drill stresses the importance of getting to the ball in order to attempt a play.

One and Two Pointers.
Two players play catch. Thrower scores 2 points if ball is caught at or above the shoulders. 1 point is awarded if caught between waist and shoulders. No points if caught below the waist or not caught. First player to score 10 points wins. This drill reinforces the importance of throwing the ball to the receiving player in such a manner that the ball can be easily caught. (This drill can also be reversed so that the receiver can be awarded two points based on successfully making the more diffcult catch.)

PRACTICE PLAN

(Put player initials in boxes above areas to be used for writing in number of repetitions of each drill. Use check boxes to indicate you did this drill.

Drill — Player Initials *																
☐ Bounce It To The Bucket																
☐ Have A Catch With A Coach																
☐ "No Dropsies" Contest																
☐ Catching Flies																
☐ Who Can Catch The Coach?																
☐ Home to 2nd/2nd to Home Relay																
☐ Crab Drill																
☐ Crow Hop																
☐ Action-Distraction-Reaction																
☐ Stretching The Play																
☐ Just Block It																
☐ One And Two Pointers																
☐ Run Down But Not Out																
☐ Scoop-Up And Throw																
☐ To First Base And Beyond																
☐ "Bulls-Eye" Drill																
☐ Hit For Distance Drill																
☐ GO! or NO! Drill																
☐ Catching Fly Balls Drill																
☐ Advancing Baserunners On Hit Balls																
☐ "No Swarm" Outfield																
☐ Fielding Balls Hit to Outfield																
☐ Running To First Base Drill																
☐ Rounding The Bases Drill																
☐ Point To Da Man																
☐ Hip-Plosion Batting Drill																
☐ Fielding FUN-damentals																
☐ Fielding Bouncing Ground Balls																
☐ Moving Ground Balls																
☐ "Bulls-Eye" Wall Toss Drill																
☐ "Under & Over" Catching Drill																

Run Down But Not Out.
This drill involves two fielders and a runner. The runner attempts to advance from one base to another without getting tagged out while staying in the baseline. The object is for the baserunner to learn to successfully avoid the tag, and for the "tagging team" to successfully tag out the runner. Participants rotate positions.

Scoop-Up & Throw.
Two players (or two rows of players) face each other about 10 feet apart. From kneeling position, one player rolls the ball to the other. The receiving player then throws the ball back to the other player. Repeat 10 to 15 times. Then switch directions. This drill accomplishes two things: 1.) It makes the player field the ball properly; 2.) It has the throwing player employ the proper throwing motion (using upper body) throwing the ball back to the other player.

PRACTICE PLAN

(Put player initials in boxes above areas to be used for writing in number of repetitions of each drill. Use check boxes to indicate you did this drill.

Drill Player Initials *													
☐ Bounce It To The Bucket													
☐ Have A Catch With A Coach													
☐ "No Dropsies" Contest													
☐ Catching Flies													
☐ Who Can Catch The Coach?													
☐ Home to 2nd/2nd to Home Relay													
☐ Crab Drill													
☐ Crow Hop													
☐ Action-Distraction-Reaction													
☐ Stretching The Play													
☐ Just Block It													
☐ One And Two Pointers													
☐ Run Down But Not Out													
☐ Scoop-Up And Throw													
☐ To First Base And Beyond													
☐ "Bulls-Eye" Drill													
☐ Hit For Distance Drill													
☐ GO! or NO! Drill													
☐ Catching Fly Balls Drill													
☐ Advancing Baserunners On Hit Balls													
☐ "No Swarm" Outfield													
☐ Fielding Balls Hit to Outfield													
☐ Running To First Base Drill													
☐ Rounding The Bases Drill													
☐ Point To Da Man													
☐ Hip-Plosion Batting Drill													
☐ Fielding FUN-damentals													
☐ Fielding Bouncing Ground Balls													
☐ Moving Ground Balls													
☐ "Bulls-Eye" Wall Toss Drill													
☐ "Under & Over" Catching Drill													

To First Base & Beyond.
Players start at home plate. At the START signal from the coach, they are instructed to run "through the base" or turn towards second. If they are to run through the base, they are instructed to give a high five to a parent helper 5 feet past the base. This drill emphasizes that the baserunner should run HARD "through (past) the base." Explain to them that those last five feet will sometimes make the difference between an out and a base hit, and that by running hard they will often beat out the throw.

"Bulls-Eye" Drill.
The batter hits into a backstop, wall or a hitting net starting from a distance of about ten feet gradually moving the tee and increasing the distance. Construct a bulls-eye target by painting circles on a square piece of cloth. Paint a bulls-eye in the center, where a level swing would produce a line drive, straight up the middle. You can assign points for hitting the bull's-eye and for hitting surrounding circles and keep score on a set of 10 hits. The purpose of this drill is to teach your players to focus on the ball and see the results of where they hit it when they concentrate.

PRACTICE PLAN

(Put player initials in boxes above areas to be used for writing in number of repetitions of each drill. Use check boxes to indicate you did this drill.

Drill Player Initials *														
☐ Bounce It To The Bucket														
☐ Have A Catch With A Coach														
☐ "No Dropsies" Contest														
☐ Catching Flies														
☐ Who Can Catch The Coach?														
☐ Home to 2nd/2nd to Home Relay														
☐ Crab Drill														
☐ Crow Hop														
☐ Action-Distraction-Reaction														
☐ Stretching The Play														
☐ Just Block It														
☐ One And Two Pointers														
☐ Run Down But Not Out														
☐ Scoop-Up And Throw														
☐ To First Base And Beyond														
☐ "Bulls-Eye" Drill														
☐ Hit For Distance Drill														
☐ GO! or NO! Drill														
☐ Catching Fly Balls Drill														
☐ Advancing Baserunners On Hit Balls														
☐ "No Swarm" Outfield														
☐ Fielding Balls Hit to Outfield														
☐ Running To First Base Drill														
☐ Rounding The Bases Drill														
☐ Point To Da Man														
☐ Hip-Plosion Batting Drill														
☐ Fielding FUN-damentals														
☐ Fielding Bouncing Ground Balls														
☐ Moving Ground Balls														
☐ "Bulls-Eye" Wall Toss Drill														
☐ "Under & Over" Catching Drill														

Hit For Distance Drill.

This drill requires a setup in which the batter hits into a baseball diamond or open field with a standard swing off the tee from home plate. Markers can be placed in the field to indicate distances from home plate, or the farthest hit can be marked and the mark only changed when a longer hit occurs. The spot should be marked where the ball hits the ground, not where it stops rolling. A variation on this drill is to line off the field for singles, doubles, triples, and home runs. The primary focus of this drill is to emphasize the importance of the player hitting the ball HARD each time.

GO! Or NO! Drill

This drill teaches the importance of watching the ball and the opposing player on a hit ball. Have a runner stand on second base. Teach them to listen closely to the coach's instructions so they can anticipate the correct action and run the bases well. Demonstrate by hitting grounders or shallow pop ups, and instruct runner as to proper action.

PRACTICE PLAN

(Put player initials in boxes above areas to be used for writing in number of repetitions of each drill. Use check boxes to indicate you did this drill.

Drill Player Initials *														
☐ Bounce It To The Bucket														
☐ Have A Catch With A Coach														
☐ "No Dropsies" Contest														
☐ Catching Flies														
☐ Who Can Catch The Coach?														
☐ Home to 2nd/2nd to Home Relay														
☐ Crab Drill														
☐ Crow Hop														
☐ Action-Distraction-Reaction														
☐ Stretching The Play														
☐ Just Block It														
☐ One And Two Pointers														
☐ Run Down But Not Out														
☐ Scoop-Up And Throw														
☐ To First Base And Beyond														
☐ "Bulls-Eye" Drill														
☐ Hit For Distance Drill														
☐ GO! or NO! Drill														
☐ Catching Fly Balls Drill														
☐ Advancing Baserunners On Hit Balls														
☐ "No Swarm" Outfield														
☐ Fielding Balls Hit to Outfield														
☐ Running To First Base Drill														
☐ Rounding The Bases Drill														
☐ Point To Da Man														
☐ Hip-Plosion Batting Drill														
☐ Fielding FUN-damentals														
☐ Fielding Bouncing Ground Balls														
☐ Moving Ground Balls														
☐ "Bulls-Eye" Wall Toss Drill														
☐ "Under & Over" Catching Drill														

INDIVIDUAL PLAYER/DRILL EVELUATION FORM

Bounce It To The Bucket.

Put a large basket or cooler on a base. Outfielders try to throw and bounce the ball to hit the target. 10 points for getting the ball in, 5 for hitting the bucket and 1 point for the nearest bounce, no matter where the ball ends up. This drill teaches throwing from the outfield to a base.

Player Name: **Comment(s)**   **Skill Level (1-5)**

INDIVIDUAL PLAYER/DRILL EVELUATION FORM

Have A Catch With A Coach.
A player and a coach (or parent helper) play catch standing approximately ten feet apart. Focus on proper throwing technique. Make a game of it and keep score of the number of successful catches. This drill teaches proper throwing and catching technique.

Player Name: **Comment(s)**   **Skill Level (1-5)**

_____

_____

_____

_____

_____

_____

_____

_____

_____

_____

_____

_____

_____

INDIVIDUAL PLAYER/DRILL EVELUATION FORM

"No Dropsies" Contest.
Players are in pairs and throw the ball back and forth between each other. If they drop a ball, their team is out. Last pair that has not dropped a ball wins. This drill teaches the players to focus on making the catch and holding onto the ball.

Player Name: **Comment(s)**   **Skill Level (1-5)**

INDIVIDUAL PLAYER/DRILL EVELUATION FORM

Catching Flies.

Hit or throw fly balls to fielders by using a soft baseball, rubber ball or tennis ball. Be sure to demonstrate the proper technique (ie: how to position the glove, how to cover the ball with the other hand etc.). How many can they catch in a row? Repetition is the key to success. This drill teaches and reinforces proper fly ball catching techniques.

Player Name: **Comment(s)**   **Skill Level (1-5)**

INDIVIDUAL PLAYER/DRILL EVELUATION FORM

Who Can Catch the Coach?
Coach runs from home plate to first base. After a few steps, coach shouts "tag me" to a player holding a ball, who runs after the coach and tries to tag him out. Coach to decide where/when/if the player attempting the tag is successful. This skill teaches pursuit until the tag is made.

Player Name: **Comment(s)**   **Skill Level (1-5)**

Home to Second/Second to Home Relay.

Coach puts half the team at home plate, the other half at second base. At the command "GO!" first player at each position runs to the other position (ie: home to second; second to home). Once the player has arrived at the next position, the next player on his team runs to the next position. This drill is continued until all players have run once. This skill develops baserunning speed.

Player Name: **Comment(s)**   **Skill Level (1-5)**

_____

_____

_____

_____

_____

_____

_____

_____

_____

_____

_____

_____

_____

Crab Drill.
Player is in basic fielding position stance - crouched forward with glove open and down. Player steps to the ball as the coach rolls the ball for them to field. Vary this by rolling the ball to one side or another, teaching them to move laterally. This drill reinforces proper fielding position and correct technique in fielding balls which move to either side of the player. (Increase the difficulty of the play attempt as the season progresses and the player improves.)

Player Name:	Comment(s)	Skill Level (1-5)

Crow Hop.
Player takes a short step and a hop in the direction of the throw, ending with the index finger pointing toward the intended target. The coach (or parent helper) throws the ball to the player, and the player throws the ball back using this method. This drill teaches proper body mechanics on the throw.

Player Name: **Comment(s)**   **Skill Level (1-5)**

_____

_____

_____

_____

_____

_____

_____

_____

_____

_____

_____

_____

_____

_____

INDIVIDUAL PLAYER/DRILL EVELUATION FORM

Action - Distraction - Reaction.
Coach rolls the ball to a fielder, but another player runs in front of the fielder and tries to break the fielder's concentration on catching the ball. If the player successfully fields the ball, he is awarded a point. The player with the most points at the end of this drill wins. This drill reinforces the importance of being focused on the ball and blocking out distractions.

Player Name: **Comment(s)**   **Skill Level (1-5)**

INDIVIDUAL PLAYER/DRILL EVELUATION FORM

Stretching The Play.
Coach throws or hits ball to one side or the other of a fielder, far
enough that he/she has to "stretch" (or move laterally) to field the
ball. Then, the fielder must throw to first base. This drill teaches
a player to "go after" a ball outside the "easy play zone" and make
the follow-up play.

Player Name: **Comment(s)**   **Skill Level (1-5)**

INDIVIDUAL PLAYER/DRILL EVELUATION FORM

Just Block It.
Coach hits ball directly to a fielder. Emphasis is on stopping the ball to keep it from getting through to the outfield. It is OK to just block the ball. This drill can be a game with a point scored for every block, two for a catch and zero if the ball is not stopped. This drill stresses the importance of getting to the ball in order to attempt a play.

Player Name: **Comment(s)**   **Skill Level (1-5)**

_____

_____

_____

_____

_____

_____

_____

_____

_____

_____

_____

_____

INDIVIDUAL PLAYER/DRILL EVELUATION FORM

One and Two Pointers.
Two players play catch. Thrower scores 2 points if ball is caught at or above the shoulders. 1 point is awarded if caught between waist and shoulders. No points if caught below the waist or not caught. First player to score 10 points wins. This drill reinforce the importance of throwing the ball to the receiving player i such a manner that the ball can be easily caught. (This drill ca also be reversed so that the receiver can be awarded two point based on successfully making the more diffcult catch.)

Player Name: **Comment(s)**   **Skill Level (1-5)**

_____

_____

_____

_____

_____

_____

_____

_____

_____

_____

_____

_____

_____

_____

INDIVIDUAL PLAYER/DRILL EVELUATION FORM

Run Down But Not Out.

This drill involves two fielders and a runner. The runner attempts to advance from one base to another without getting tagged out while staying in the baseline. The object is for the baserunner to learn to successfully avoid the tag, and for the "tagging team" to successfully tag out the runner. Participants rotate positions.

Player Name: **Comment(s)**   **Skill Level (1-5)**

_____

_____

_____

_____

_____

_____

_____

_____

_____

_____

_____

_____

_____

INDIVIDUAL PLAYER/DRILL EVELUATION FORM

Scoop-Up & Throw.

Two players (or two rows of players) face each other about 10 fee apart. From kneeling position, one player rolls the ball to the othe The receiving player then throws the ball back to the other playe Repeat 10 to 15 times. Then switch directions. This drill accom plishes two things: 1.) It makes the player field the ball properly 2.) It has the throwing player employ the proper throwing motio (using upper body) throwing the ball back to the other player.

Player Name: **Comment(s)**   **Skill Level (1-5)**

_____

_____

_____

_____

_____

_____

_____

_____

_____

_____

_____

_____

_____

INDIVIDUAL PLAYER/DRILL EVELUATION FORM

To First Base & Beyond.
Players start at home plate. At the START signal from the coach, they are instructed to run "through the base" or turn towards second. If they are to run through the base, they are instructed to give a high five to a parent helper 5 feet past the base. This drill emphasizes that the baserunner should run HARD "through (past) the base." Explain to them that those last five feet will sometimes make the difference between an out and a base hit, and that by running hard they will often beat out the throw.

Player Name: **Comment(s)**   **Skill Level (1-5)**

_____

_____

_____

_____

_____

_____

_____

_____

_____

_____

_____

_____

_____

_____

"Bulls-Eye" Drill.

The batter hits into a backstop, wall or a hitting net starting from a distance of about ten feet gradually moving the tee and increasing the distance. Construct a bulls-eye target by painting circles on a square piece of cloth. Paint a bulls-eye in the center, where a level swing would produce a line drive, straight up the middle. You can assign points for hitting the bull's-eye and for hitting surrounding circles and keep score on a set of 10 hits. The purpose of this drill is to teach your players to focus on the ball and see the results of where they hit it when they concentrate.

Player Name: **Comment(s)**   **Skill Level (1-5)**

_____

_____

_____

_____

_____

_____

_____

_____

_____

_____

_____

_____

_____

Hit For Distance Drill.

This drill requires a setup in which the batter hits into a baseball diamond or open field with a standard swing off the tee from home plate. Markers can be placed in the field to indicate distances from home plate, or the farthest hit can be marked and the mark only changed when a longer hit occurs. The spot should be marked where the ball hits the ground, not where it stops rolling. A variation on this drill is to line off the field for singles, doubles, triples, and home runs. The primary focus of this drill is to emphasize the importance of the player hitting the ball HARD each time.

Player Name: **Comment(s)**   **Skill Level (1-5)**

GO! Or NO! Drill

This drill teaches the importance of watching the ball and the op
posing player on a hit ball. Have a runner stand on second base
Teach them to listen closely to the coach's instructions so they ca
anticipate the correct action and run the bases well. Demonstrat
by hitting grounders or shallow pop ups, and instruct runner as t
proper action.

Player Name: **Comment(s)**   **Skill Level (1-5)**

ENCOURAGE PRACTICE AT HOME

Practice time is at a premium. Most teams get 4-5 practices(at most!) before the season starts lasting an hour to an hour and fifteen minutes at best. Coaching a team comprised of energetic 4-6 year olds with varying skill levels is a definite challenge. There simply isn't time to cover everything you need and want to cover in the time you will have available.

The next best thing to practice as a team is individual skill-building done at home between organized practices. A great way to encourage this is to hand out Player Contracts to players for them to fulfill between practices. The Player Contracts are a short list (3 to 5 at most) of drills that can be done with dad, mom, siblings, grandparents, etc. These drills should be done for a specified number of repetitions each day. The drills are explained on the contract, and there is a place for the player AND the parent to sign before bringing it to the next practice. If the completed form is returned to the coach indicating that the player has successfully completed the terms of his contract, the player then receives a **BONUS** for completing the contract. The Bonus should be something tangible the player receives (ie: a pack of baseball cards, a star on their cap, a coupon for an ice cream cone, etc.). Do **NOT** give bonuses to players who do not complete the requirements as this will negate the value of the practice. Each player will then have another chance to successfully meet their bonus requirements before the next practice. **Try this - it really works!!**

- -

PLANNING A SUCCESSFUL PRACTICE

Let's repeat it. Practice time is at a premium.

The greatest disservice you can do to the players on your team, their parents and yourself, is to be disorganized when it comes to practice and game time. On the next few pages are practice formats with check boxes to organize your practice times and get the most out of your time and your players. While it would be impossible to get all of these drills done in a single practice, you can probably implement 6 to 7 in an hour and a half practice session.

Stations. The optimum way to get the most done in a practice session is break the field into 4 stations with each player at a station simultaneously doing the drills and rotating between the stations during the practice period (Obviously, you're going to need lots of parent helpers). For example, have them at each station for ten minutes - then rotate. In 40 minutes, each child has done 4 drills. The remainder of the practice can be done utilizing 3 other drills of your choosing in 10 minute increments and finish up with a purely fun game such as a race from home to second and second to home.

Once you feel the youngsters have mastered a skill, rotate that drill with another to develop or enhance additional skills.

Progress Evaluations. On the pages following the practice outlines are a series of forms with plenty of spaces for player progress evaluations. On these sheets you should write an ongoing evaluation of your players and how they are mastering their skills during your practice sessions in the course of the season. Make a separate copy of each sheet for each player and keep it in your coach's notebook.

(Blank Drill Sheet for Setting up your own combination of drills for a practice)

PRACTICE PLAN

(Put player initials in boxes above areas to be used for writing in number of repetitions of each drill. Use check boxes to indicate you did this drill.

Drill Player Initials *														
☐ Bounce It To The Bucket														
☐ Have A Catch With A Coach														
☐ "No Dropsies" Contest														
☐ Catching Flies														
☐ Who Can Catch The Coach?														
☐ Home to 2nd/2nd to Home Relay														
☐ Crab Drill														
☐ Crow Hop														
☐ Action-Distraction-Reaction														
☐ Stretching The Play														
☐ Just Block It														
☐ One And Two Pointers														
☐ Run Down But Not Out														
☐ Scoop-Up And Throw														
☐ To First Base And Beyond														
☐ "Bulls-Eye" Drill														
☐ Hit For Distance Drill														
☐ GO! or NO! Drill														
☐ Catching Fly Balls Drill														
☐ Advancing Baserunners On Hit Balls														
☐ "No Swarm" Outfield														
☐ Fielding Balls Hit to Outfield														
☐ Running To First Base Drill														
☐ Rounding The Bases Drill														
☐ Point To Da Man														
☐ Hip-Plosion Batting Drill														
☐ Fielding FUN-damentals														
☐ Fielding Bouncing Ground Balls														
☐ Moving Ground Balls														
☐ "Bulls-Eye" Wall Toss Drill														
☐ "Under & Over" Catching Drill														

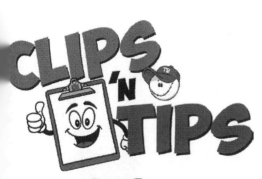

PLAYER PROGRESS EVALUATION

COACH'S NOTES:

_____
_____
_____
_____
_____
_____
_____
_____

PRACTICE PLAN	Give your player numerical rankings below on any given drill. There are multiple boxes so you can show the player's progress numerically during the course of the season.

Drill (PLAYER NAME: _____)														
☐ Bounce It To The Bucket														
☐ Have A Catch With A Coach														
☐ "No Dropsies" Contest														
☐ Catching Flies														
☐ Who Can Catch The Coach?														
☐ Home to 2nd/2nd to Home Relay														
☐ Crab Drill														
☐ Crow Hop														
☐ Action-Distraction-Reaction														
☐ Stretching The Play														
☐ Just Block It														
☐ One And Two Pointers														
☐ Run Down But Not Out														
☐ Scoop-Up And Throw														
☐ To First Base And Beyond														
☐ "Bulls-Eye" Drill														
☐ Hit For Distance Drill														
☐ GO! or NO! Drill														
☐ Catching Fly Balls Drill														
☐ Advancing Baserunners On Hit Balls														
☐ "No Swarm" Outfield														
☐ Fielding Balls Hit to Outfield														
☐ Running To First Base Drill														
☐ Rounding The Bases Drill														
☐ Point To Da Man														
☐ Hip-Plosion Batting Drill														
☐ Fielding FUN-damentals														
☐ Fielding Bouncing Ground Balls														
☐ Moving Ground Balls														
☐ "Bulls-Eye" Wall Toss Drill														
☐ "Under & Over" Catching Drill														

KEEP IT IN PERSPECTIVE

Tee Ball is the first step in organized baseball for young players. Tee ball is the building block of the future of Youth League and High School teams. Teaching the proper mechanics will give a child confidence on and off the field. As a coach and as a parent, you are responsible to pass as much good information as possible. You are also responsible for instilling either a positive or negative attitude towards the game in these young players.

Our culture bombards us with the concept that winning is everything. While teaching to play your best is important, youth sports are different from professional sports. Professional athletics is about winning games and making money. Youth athletics is about having fun **(FIRST & FOREMOST!)**, improving skills, developing character and making a lifetime commitment to physical activity.

Kids who always feel pressured to win will most probably "drop out" sooner rather than later. Kids play sports mainly to have fun and be with their friends. Winning is way down on their list. Most kids would rather be active participants on a losing team, than sit on the bench of a winning one.

Tee Ball is for young players to have fun, learn, participate, and prepare for the next level of play.

TeeBall-To-A-Tee's unique Clips 'N Tips System © is a perfect combination with the "TeeBall Coaching Handbook" which you purchased together with the Clips 'N Tips System ©. Combining the two in a Coach's Notebook 3-ring binder is the ideal way to use the two together to enhance the teeball coaching experience!

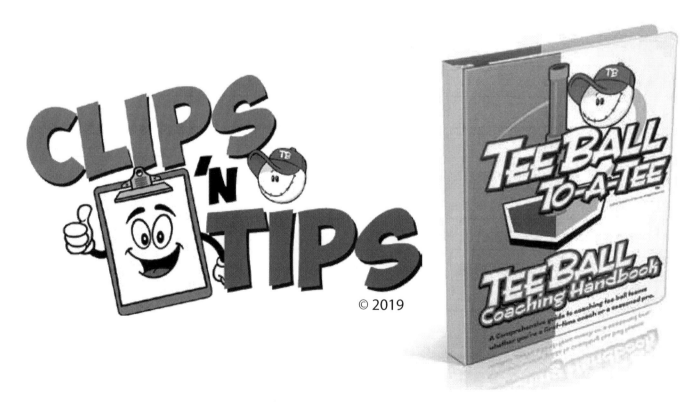

© 2019

Made in the USA
Columbia, SC
13 February 2019